Shopping malls

Planning and design

Shopping malls:
planning and design

Barry Maitland

NICHOLS

Construction Press
an imprint of.
Longman Group Limited
Longman House, Burnt Mill, Harlow
Essex CM20 2JE, England
Associated companies throughout the world

First published in the United States
of America in 1985 by
Nichols Publishing Company
Post Office Box 96
New York N.Y. 10024

First published 1985

Library of Congress Cataloging in Publication Data
Maitland, Barry
  Shopping malls.
  Bibliography: p.
  Includes index.
    1. Shopping malls—Planning. 2. Shopping malls—
Designs and plans. I. Title.
NA6218. M34 1985   711′.5522   85–7297

ISBN 0-89397-226-6

Set in 10/11 Linotron 202 Times Roman.
Printed in Great Britain at
The Bath Press, Avon

Contents

Acknowledgements

I am greatly indebted to the Leverhulme Trust for a research grant which enabled me to visit most of the North American centres referred to here, during 1981. I am also most grateful to the University of Sheffield for study grants which enabled me to carry out research on the morphology of medieval towns in Germany and Italy referred to in Chapter 7.

It would be impossible to write a book of this kind without the support of practitioners in the architectural and planning professions, who are willing to interrupt the daily battle to provide information, drawings, photographs and opinions to an author. I would thank all those who have helped me in this way, including: Richard Young of Sheppard Robson; Keith Maplestone of Peterborough Development Corporation; Nigel Woolner of Chapman Taylor Partners; Bregman and Hamann; George Hoare of Grosvenor Estate Commercial Developments Ltd; Richard Francaviglia; Marc Rector of Benjamin Thompson Associates; Ross L. Davies; Bill Dahl of Gruen Associates; Buz Golightly; Keith Scott, Sheri Besford and Chris Sayers of Buildings Design Partnership; Gino Rossetti of Rossetti Associates; Aaron Chelouche of Lathrop Douglass–Aaron Chelouche; John S. Bonnington of John S. Bonnington Partnership; John Abel; Dan Sinclair of the City of Calgary; Lyle Balderson of the City of Spokane; Efraim S. Garcia of the City of Houston; City Planning Department of the City of Minneapolis; Harry Seidler of Harry Seidler Associates; Mark McKillip of the City of Cincinnati; Jes Wolf of the International Council of Shopping Centers, New York; Planning Department of the City of Leeds; the City of Coventry; Claude Vasconi of Vasconi–Pencreac'h; John Pringle of Michael Hopkins Architects; Michael Wilford of James Stirling, Michael Wilford and Associates; and to all of the centre managers who gave me help, information and permission to photograph their centres.

Finally, I am indebted to the competence of my typists, Ruth Barker and Kath Barber; to the patience of my publishers, and in particular Colin Bassett and Bobbi Gouge; and to the long-sufferance of my family, Sarah, James and Clare.

Note on scales

In a book of this kind, where many buildings of similar type are being reviewed, a comparative basis for that examination is important. For this reason, plans and sections have been generally redrawn throughout to common scales as follows:

Mall sections	1 : 300
Wider building sections	1 : 600
Building plans	1 : 3,000
Town and development structure plans	1 : 12,000

To my parents

James Maitland 1906–1961
Mary Maitland 1907–1983

Chapter 1 Introduction

The retailing function of the city has always provided some of its most memorable and interesting places. Whether encrusting the frontages of its main streets, as at Pompeii [1.1]* or filling the market squares of medieval towns [1.2] or condensed along an enclosed thoroughfare as in the Isfahan bazaar [1.3] coiling through the city like a digestive tract, it has traditionally offered the most concentrated expression of informal public life, counterbalancing the formal civic spaces of forum and *maidan*. And, perhaps more than any other single use in the city, it has been instrumental in creating novel and ingenious hardware for the definition, protection and enclosure of public space.

But if these characteristics of retailing were apparent in the historical city, and were substantially reaffirmed with the nineteenth-century developments of the arcade, department store and covered market hall, their significance has been dramatically heightened by the events of the past thirty years. The sheer profusion of new shopping facilities created during this period, both in terms of their numbers and in their variety of rapidly evolving types, has been unprecedented in the history of the city. By 1980 the URPI Register of Managed Shopping Schemes[1] could list 600 such centres which had been built in Britain since the Second World War, of which 227 provided more than 10,000 sq. metres of gross leasable area (GLA), while in Europe 195 regional centres, at over 28,000 sq. metres GLA, had been completed by that date.[2] In North America their growth was even more spectacular, with 1,650 centres of all sizes and types being added in the US in that year alone to a total which then exceeded 20,000,[3] of which some 1,700 were major regionals.[4]

Yet despite this extraordinary growth, and the highly accessible and public nature of the building type, it has received very little critical attention.

* Italic numerals in square brackets refer to the illustrations.

1

1.1   Distribution of shopping facilities (solid black) in
Roman Pompeii. 1 : 12,000.

1.2   Street market in Soest, Germany.

Books have been written on its technical and
operational aspects, and studies undertaken on its
planning implications, particularly those relating to
location, but in terms of its architectural
development and its physical impact upon
contemporary urban development, the literature of
post-war architectural criticism and analysis has
been curiously silent.

There are a number of reasons why this might be
so. In the first place, the building type underwent
very little development during the period between
the two World Wars when the central philosophies
of post-war architecture and planning were formed,
and in the seminal projects of the Modern
Movement it figured, if at all, as a marginal
element beside the major urban functions of
housing, offices, factories, and educational,
recreational and cultural institutions. It may be that
the diverse and capitalist nature of retailing was out
of key with the spirit of public enterprise which

2

1.3   The covered bazaar at Isfahan, Iran. Exterior of covered street winding through the city.

informed those projects, and which hardly anticipated the role of the private developer in post-war urban development. Certainly as an architectural problem the shopping mall is highly fluid and contingent, continuously obliged to pursue the subject rather than the object of design, to accommodate a shifting and expedient brief rather than a platonic formal idea. Again, the architects who have designed these buildings have tended to specialise in this field and, with a few such exceptions as Eric Mendelsohn before the Second World War and Cesar Pelli after, have been relatively unknown outside of it.

Whatever the reasons, however, it is difficult to avoid a conclusion similar to that voiced by Richard Francaviglia (1974: 10), an American urban geographer, in relation to his own profession, that 'a strange kind of moralistic fervour has kept geographers from studying the new shopping centers, which are supposed to be "blah", plastic and contrived. And they may be. But they are successful. And in their success lies a clue: not that they are good or bad, but rather that they are working as designed.'

Often gaudy and 'popular' in their architectural taste, and compromised in their architectonic resolution, it would nevertheless seem as improbable to write a social or architectural history of mid twentieth-century America without reference to these buildings as to discuss Victorian England without mention of its great railway termini. Pursuing their own logic of development and responding to the continually changing demographic patterns of post-war Europe and North America, they now amount to a formidable transformation of the character of built public space in the city as it is perceived by most of its inhabitants. This book attempts a limited appraisal of that transformation in two ways: first by considering the form of the shopping mall as it has evolved in Europe and North America over the past thirty years, and particularly in its later stages; and then, in the second part of the book, by looking at some of the implications which this development has created for the cities in which it has occurred. Given the great numbers of examples available, the study could not hope to be comprehensive, and a selection has been made of those projects which best seemed to illustrate the main lines of development or else to provide interesting variations upon them. Despite these limitations it may contribute to a broader analysis of an extraordinary period of development in Western cities, and of one key agent in that development, the urban mall, which, in its prolific variety of built form and radical planning drift, can hardly be ignored in any consideration of the directions which that development may now take.

Notes

1. *Register of UK Managed Shopping Schemes, URPI P3.* The Unit for Retail Planning Information Ltd, London 1980.

   For an analysis of the content and background to 184 of these schemes, see Davies, R. L. and Bennison, D. J., 1979.

2. Figure cited by H. M. D. Norton in a paper *Review of Shopping Centre Development in Continental Europe in 1982* to International Council of Shopping Centers Conference, Monte Carlo 1983.

3. Figure cited by M. F. Gaskie in 'Shopping centers', *Architectural Record*, Apr. 1982: 124.

4. H. M. D. Norton, op. cit.

Part 1: The mall as form-type

Chapter 2 The invention of
the industrialised mall

It must seem extraordinary that the development of the glazed shopping arcade [2.1], sustained for over 100 years, should have come to such an abrupt conclusion in the early years of the twentieth century. While other inventions of nineteenth-century urbanism – the transport interchange and framed office tower for example – were absorbed

2.1 Barton Arcade, Manchester, 1871: interior view.

into the mythologies of Futurism, Expressionism and the New Objectivity, to emerge as key components of the Ville Radieuse, the arcade was relegated to obsolescence. Receiving a final acknowledgement in Ebenezer Howard's Garden City plan, as the annular centre-piece of the town, surrounding its central park, it then disappeared, and with it almost all references to the retailing function as a significant urban element.

In terms of actual production this disregard must have seemed justified, for as far as shopping was concerned, new city developments largely took the form of individual buildings, modest in comparison with their Victorian antecedents and innovatory only in their adoption of the external modernism inspired by Eric Mendelsohn's series of German department stores, while conventionally arranged parades of new shops were constructed in the expanding suburbs. And when the needs of post-war expansion brought this period of hibernation to an end, and created once more the opportunity for shopping to figure as an integral element of urban reconstruction, the Victorian notion of the arcade as a coherent spatial element was at first entirely absent.

In part this may be attributed to the determination of progressive planning thought to abandon the 'corridor-street' as a physical element and organising principle of the city, and instead regard its functions as housed in discrete pavilions set in open space, across which rationally disposed circulation systems would operate. Le Corbusier's 1945 plan for the reconstruction of the central area of Saint-Dié [2.2] exemplifies this attitude. 'Grands Magasins' are accommodated in a single building block which, along with those for other designated uses of the central area – culture, administration, sport and so on – sits on an extensive open pedestrian podium. This figure-ground reversal of the pattern of solid and void in the traditional city, which effectively denies the possibility of public circulation space as a contained form alongside that of the buildings it serves, was also adopted in the new shopping centres which emerged in North America at this time, though for a rather different set of reasons.

Responding to a major demographic shift out of the developed city areas, encouraged by new highway programmes and house-purchase grants to returning GIs, these new centres occupied huge

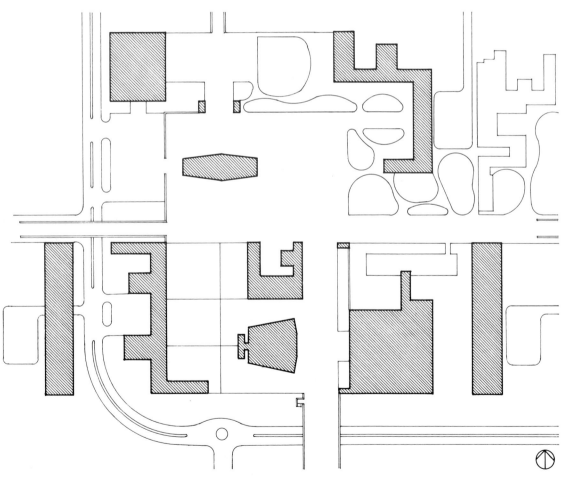

2.2 Saint-Dié, France: Le Corbusier's plan for the
reconstruction of the centre of the city, 1945.
1 : 3,000.

green-field sites in which the traditional constraints of adjoining uses, plot form, urban density and circulation patterns were entirely removed. In considering how one might design a city's shopping component when detached from its traditional context in this way, the architects came to conclusions which echoed the principles of elemental CIAM planning, but now for commercial reasons. Victor Gruen and Larry Smith, perhaps the most prolific of these designers, set out the basis of this thinking as follows (Gruen and Smith 1960:140):

The shopping center . . . is the expression of a rare occurrence in our free enterprise economy – the banding together of individual businesses in co-operative fashion with the aim of creating greater commercial effectiveness through unified endeavour. . . .

One might compare the organization of a shopping center with the governmental structure of the United States. A strong federal government represents the country as a whole and expresses those concepts and functions which must be exercised for the good of all. Yet, within this federal framework, free expression in many essential matters has been reserved by the individual states. The overall character of the center must be one of corporate strength through the strength of the individuals. . . .

Its building group and related spaces are not strung along existing roads but constitute a new planning pattern of their own.

The first attempts to define this pattern were varied, and showed a considerable looseness in the relationship of the 'federation' of individual pavilion buildings to each other and to their related pedestrian spaces, which, Gruen and Smith calculated, could amount to an area equal to that of the gross building area itself (Gruen and Smith 1960:89). The plan for a projected centre at Toledo, Ohio, for example [2.3] grouped the buildings around an open triangular court, while others, such as the 100,000-sq. metre Old Orchard Center at Skokie, Illinois [2.4], by Loebl, Schlossman and Bennett, arranged the building pavilions about a loose network of pedestrian spaces, described for the first time in such schemes as 'malls'. The nature of the malls, as essentially open spaces formed between irregularly disposed pavilions, is common to most of these developments of the 1950s, as in one of the regional centres, Northland [2.5] which Victor Gruen Associates designed for Detroit, Michigan, in which the character of the centre as a campus of rectangular pavilions is clear.

More important than the shape of the pedestrian spaces in these projects was the set of rules which governed the federation of individual traders in order to maximise 'commercial effectiveness'. This was based upon an appreciation of the different characteristics of the component parts, some being large space-users with high turnover and acting as a major draw for visitors, while others were more specialised and dependent on the passing traffic created by the larger units. A 'merchandising plan' could thus be devised in which the primary units,

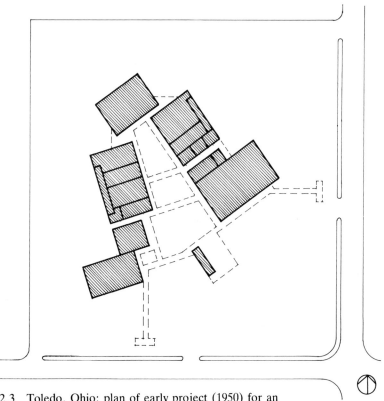

2.3   Toledo, Ohio: plan of early project (1950) for an out-of-town centre. 1 : 3,000.

or 'magnet' stores, would be so disposed that visitors to them would be led past secondary units, so maximising trading opportunities, turnover and hence rental levels, for the centre as a whole. Ultimately the logic of merchandising planning, with its mechanistic terminology of 'magnets', 'generators', 'pull' and 'flow', and its quantification of the successful plan in terms of rental yield, led to a simplification of planning patterns into a number of generic types based upon the number of major magnets, usually department stores, to be incorporated. Thus a centre with a single magnet,

such as the Northland Center, would adopt a centripetal form, with incoming shoppers from the surrounding parking areas drawn down approach malls to the central store. Since only a proportion of the incoming traffic would pass down any one approach mall, these would be kept short, with the secondary traders concentrated as far as possible around the central core area where all shoppers might be expected to circulate.

A much greater area of prime frontage for secondary traders could be created with two magnets, located at each end of a 'dumb-bell' plan

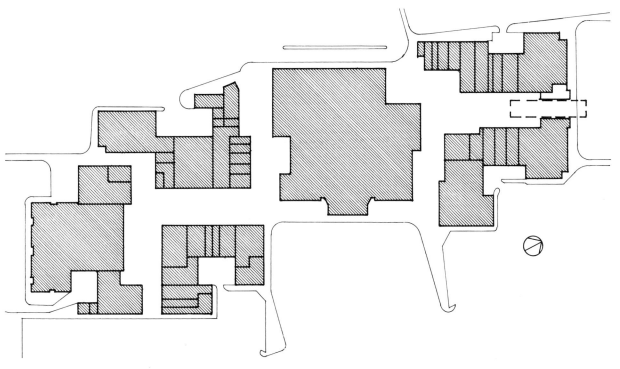

2.4   Old Orchard, Skokie, Illinois: plan. 1 : 3,000.

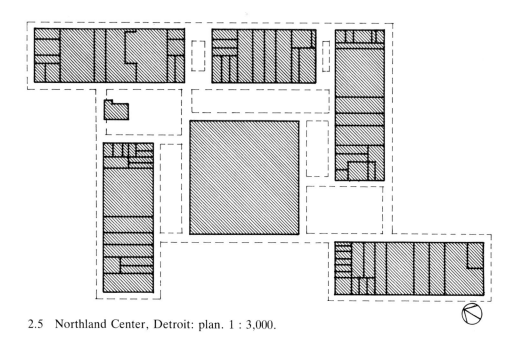

2.5   Northland Center, Detroit: plan. 1 : 3,000.

with a central mall down which shoppers would be drawn, as in the Mayfair Shopping Center, at Milwaukee, Wisconsin [2.6], in which the two department stores, Gimbel's and Field's, accounted for 55 per cent of the total retail area. In the same way, three department stores could induce a linear or a 'T' or 'L' shaped primary mall route, and four magnets a cruciform. And as these principles became clarified, so the pattern of circulation space was tightened and the mall came increasingly to adopt the simple linear form of a street, perhaps 15 metres wide, with projecting canopies from the flanking stores and areas of planting and seating in the middle [2.7].

Thus the American out-of-town shopping centre, divorced from any possibility of an urban context not only by its suburban location but also by being surrounded by 40 hectares and more of surface car parks, came, in this first stage of its development, to define the public mall as essentially the passive outcome of a merchandising plan, a channel for the manipulation of pedestrian flows. In the competitive North American situation, however, in which shopping centres rapidly came to vie with

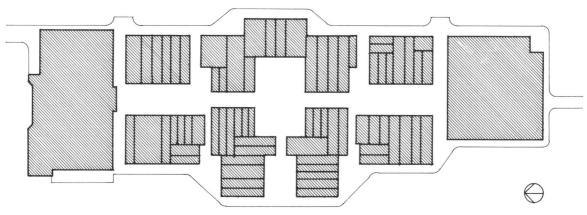

2.6   Mayfair, Milwaukee, Wisconsin: plan. 1 : 3,000.

2.7   Century Square Shopping Center, Los Angeles:
view of characteristic open mall.

10

one another in terms of comfort and convenience as much as cost, developments soon occurred in which the public space itself became, if not quite a marketable commodity, at least a major marketing attraction for the retail areas it served.

The climate in Minnesota has a temperature range from −30 °C in the winter to +42 °C in summer, and in these circumstances any shopping centre which is able to provide climate control to its malls as well as its shops must not only improve its internal circulation flows but also attract customers at the expense of competing, unprotected centres. Such was the case with Gruen's Southdale Center, outside Minneapolis, which in 1956 incorporated the first fully enclosed shopping mall in North America. Already, with this example, a number of distinctive features of future stages in

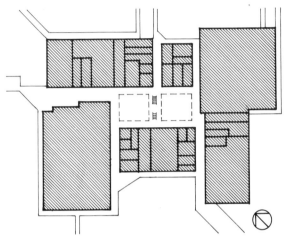

2.8 Southdale Center, Edina, Minnesota: plan. 1 : 3,000.

the development of the regional centre were introduced, and to a considerable level of sophistication.

Firstly, with respect to its plan, the upgrading of the mall area to standards approaching the retail spaces, introduced new capital and running costs to the development which in turn created pressure for a greater compactness and efficiency in plan form. This tendency was reinforced by the increasing size of such centres and the enormous land-take they required, and by a growing awareness of the reluctance of shoppers to walk great distances between magnet stores. A decisive improvement in this respect was achieved at Southdale by the creation of two superimposed trading levels, through which the central mall space, or 'Garden Court', rises. Each of these levels is served equally from the surrounding car parks by the expedient of grading them so that one-half of the site feeds the lower level, and the other the higher. Servicing to both storeys is provided by a basement storey approached by truck ramps, a common feature of the first-stage centres which tended to be abandoned on cost grounds with later schemes.

The compression of overall plan form achieved by the two-storey solution is seen in the compact mall arrangement at Southdale [2.8] in which the central Garden Court stretches between the two magnet stores, with short side malls running out to the car parks. The section of this court [2.9] is again characteristic, with a light steel roof structure spanning the space and raised above the roof level of the adjoining shops to allow clerestory natural lighting into the mall.

A further innovation at Southdale lay in the approach to mechanical services in the centre. The conventional arrangement adopted in American centres at that time was for the developer to supply

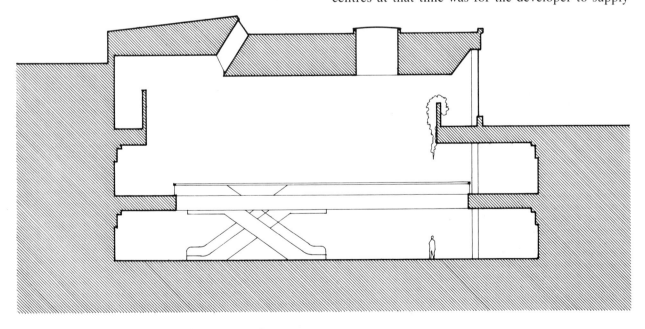

2.9 Southdale Center, Edina, Minnesota: section through Garden Court. 1 : 300.

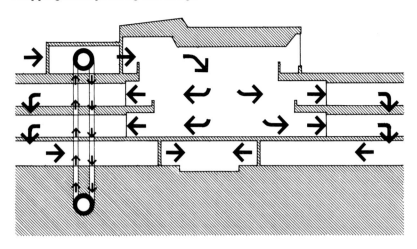

2.10 Southdale Center, Edina, Minnesota: section
     illustrating distribution of conditioned air through
     the centre. 1 : 600.

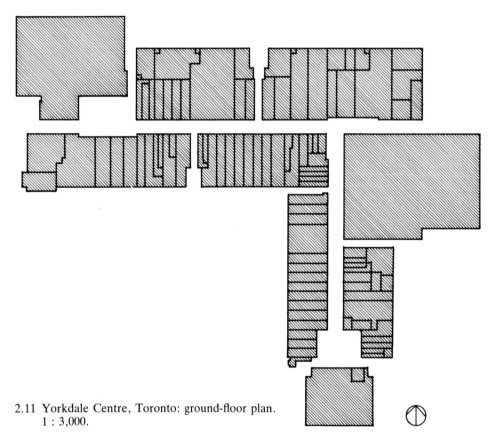

2.11 Yorkdale Centre, Toronto: ground-floor plan.
     1 : 3,000.

heating to each tenancy, but not air conditioning,
which was undertaken individually by tenants as
required. With the enclosure of the mall the energy
balance of the complex was altered and the
possibility of centralised plant for all spaces,
common and private, introduced. Such a solution
was adopted at Southdale, where it was found that
the heat generated by occupants and lighting within
the compact envelope would require cooling even
in the winter cycle. Plant located at roof level
[2.10] introduced conditioned air into the central
mall, from which it was drawn through fascia grilles

into shop units and exhausted at the rear of the
units into their common service access corridor.
From there the air passed through the basement
areas to provide secondary cooling, and thence into
the service tunnel to be exhausted with the vehicle
fumes. Water for the central plant room was drawn
from underground glacial strata in the winter at
about 27 °C to pre-heat the incoming air to the
mall, while in summer a reverse cycle was used,
with water at 50 °C from the cooling plant diffused
back into the natural reservoir.

Finally, the enclosure of the mall made it

possible to regard it as a major source of attraction in its own right, rather than simply a gap between stores, and this opportunity was grasped at Southdale with the introduction of a children's zoo, eating areas and, in 1958, the staging of the annual Minneapolis Symphony Ball in the Garden Court. The mall had thus become the focus of the marketing of the centre as a whole.

With the opening of the Southdale Center then, all of the components had been assembled which would transform the concept of the shopping centre from that of an expedient federation of individual stores into that of a single packaged entity, capable of endless reproduction in a number of set variations under any climatic conditions, and according to a well-defined process which ran from initial merchandising plan and site selection right through to final marketing and promotion. The shopping centre had become, in effect, an industrialised product, and the development industry set about equipping the cities of first North America, and then Europe, Australia, Japan, Central and South America and finally the Middle East, with this product, as each country in its turn achieved car ownership levels, at about one car per ten people, which would sustain it.

The rules which governed the mall form of the industrialised centre were generally held to include a simplicity, even rigidity of alignment, in order that shop-fronts should be as clearly visible to the greatest number of passing shoppers as possible. Coupled with this was the need to articulate the length of the mall, to sustain the interest and hence extend the flow of visitors. It was widely considered that magnet stores should not be located more than 200 metres apart, or else the flow would break down into separate circuits, and squares or courts were often introduced into the public spaces at similar intervals to relieve the visual monotony of the uninterrupted mall perspective. The Yorkdale Centre [2.11], located on the motorway network running through the northern suburbs of Toronto, provided a classic illustration of these rules. Three magnet stores, Simpson's and Eaton's department stores and a Dominion Supermarket, occupy the ends and corner of an 'L' shaped plan. The central mall is articulated by courts – Simpson's Court, Eaton's Court and Bazaar Court – corresponding to these locations and centred almost exactly 200 metres apart. Between these courts, which rise to the two-storey height of the department stores, the mall adopts the simple profile of a roofed pedestrian street [2.12], with a ceiling height raised to permit a high level of natural lighting from clerestory windows [2.13].

The 'L' shaped, three-magnet centre plan of Yorkdale constituted one of the classic variants of the industrialised centre, and was adopted from Texas (North Park, Dallas) to Quebec (le Carrefour Laval, Montreal). In the case of the North Park Center, secondary squares were introduced between the 200-metre poles at the

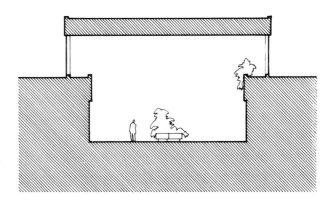

2.12 Yorkdale Centre, Toronto: section through mall 1 : 300.

point of entry of side malls. This building had the largest air-conditioned mall area of any centre at the time of its opening in 1964, and a contemporary description (*Architectural Record*, Apr. 1966) emphasised the shift in perception of the mall from the earlier, open schemes:

Not a 'street of stores' but a flowing series of naturally lighted plazas is the enclosed mall of North Park. There are six such plazas, each with direct access from parking. The three largest, with programmed fountains and plantings, mark the entrances to major stores but also provide visual contact with mall fronts of standard tenants. Turning the 'L' are two contiguous plazas which break the long vistas.

As the enclosed mall was developed, some criticisms of the early schemes were mooted. The high natural lighting levels at Yorkdale for example were felt to detract from the artificially lit shop-fronts, while the 15-metre-wide malls were thought to be too wide, discouraging shoppers from crossing from side to side. Regarding mall widths, it was generally considered that a clear 3-metre-wide circulation zone was necessary outside each shop-front giving a minimum overall mall width of about 6 metres. To this a central zone could be added for seating, planters and other features, of variable width but usually about 3 metres again for a single-storey mall.

The result of these criticisms was to move increasingly towards a tighter and totally artificially lit mall form, perhaps with some relief in ceiling height and natural lighting features over the intermittent squares. This tendency, coupled with a general preference for the more compact two-storey arrangement, characterised the larger American centres designed in the 1960s, and is demonstrated by two from many possible examples, which further illustrate classic two-magnet and four-magnet plans. Fairview Mall in Toronto has a dumb-bell layout with two department stores, Simpson's and The Bay, between which a straight main mall, 21 metres wide and 160 metres long, extends [2.14]. The upper mall level has three large openings to the lower level, in which stairs, a travelator and

2.13 Yorkdale Centre, Toronto: view of mall.

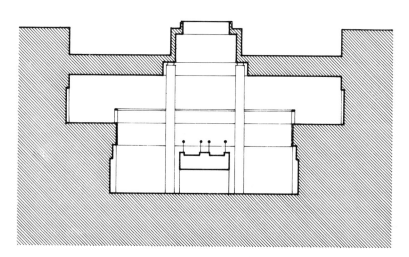

2.14 Fairview Mall, Toronto: section through central
mall. 1 : 300.

fountains are located [2.15] and rooflights over
these spaces introduce some limited natural
lighting. In contrast to the relative generosity of the
central mall space, 7.5-metre-wide side malls
penetrate the banks of shops on either side, 45 and
50 metres deep, to the car parks beyond.

In the second example, the Lakehurst Center at
Waukegan outside Chicago [2.16], a suspended
ceiling grid extends over the whole public area, at

the heart of which lies a two-storey central square
from which malls pin-wheel out to the four magnet
stores [2.17; 2.18]. The surrounding car parking
area is divided into four quadrants, which
alternately feed upper and lower mall levels of the
cruciform plan.

It would be misleading to describe the
subsequent development of the shopping mall
purely in terms of the dissemination of these North

2.15 Fairview Mall, Toronto: view of central mall.

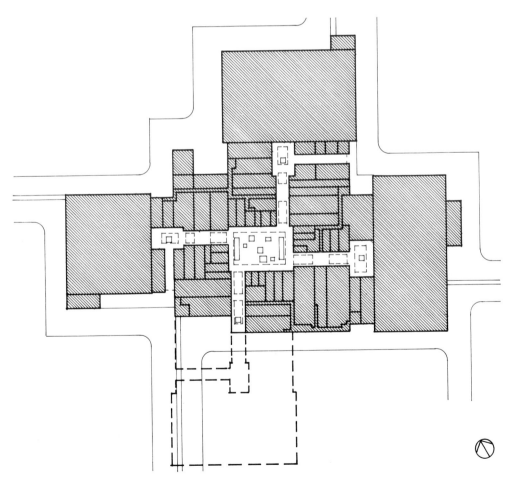

2.16 Lakehurst Center, Waukegan, Illinois: lower-level
    plan. 1 : 3,000.

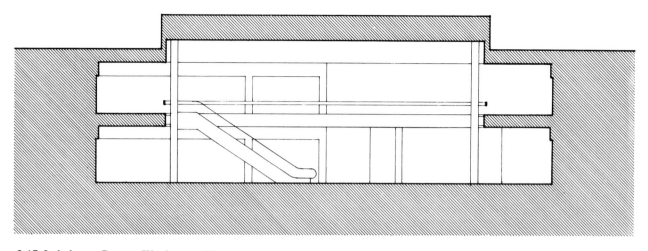

2.17 Lakehurst Center, Waukegan, Illinois: section
through central square. 1 : 300.

2.18 Lakehurst Center, Waukegan, Illinois: view of
central square.

American models, for indigenous developments took place in Europe during the post-war years, either reconstructing war-damaged centres or in New Towns, which often paralleled the American experiments. Gruen acknowledged the precinct centres formed on the Lijnbaan in Rotterdam, at Vallingby in Sweden and at Harlow in England in his book (Gruen and Smith 1960:13), and one can identify in such examples the exploration of solutions similar to those described in the first, open American centres. The cruciform plan arrangement at Coventry [2.19] multiplicity of secondary malls at Harlow [2.20], and free precinct form at Farsta [2.21], all evoke such parallels. Again, the Europeans took up the possibility of multi-level shopping, tentatively at Coventry, successfully in the Whitgift Centre at Croydon, where each level was fed directly from adjoining streets on a cross-fall site, and more problematically at the Elephant and Castle, which provided an object lesson in the difficulties of sustaining three trading levels not directly fed by incoming shoppers.

But these European examples were all designed as the physical centres of continuous urban development, and it is impossible to discuss their

2.19 Coventry: view of central precinct. (Courtesy City of Coventry)

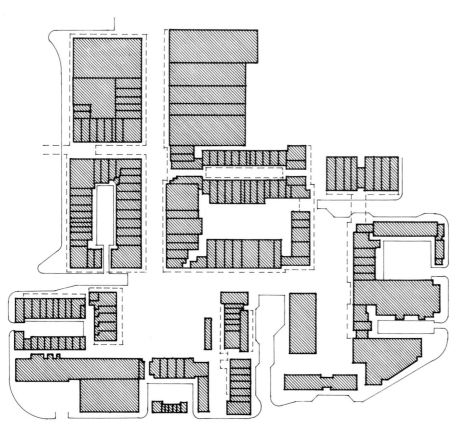

2.20 Harlow New Town: plan of first phases of central shopping area. 1 : 3,000.

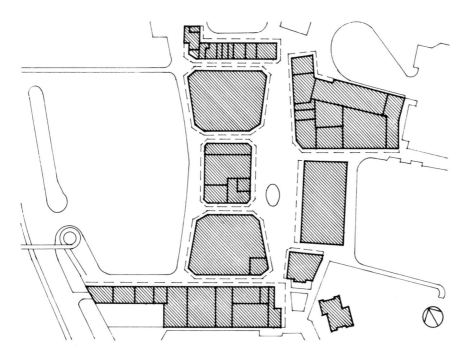

2.21 Farsta New Town, Stockholm: plan of central shopping area. 1 : 3,000.

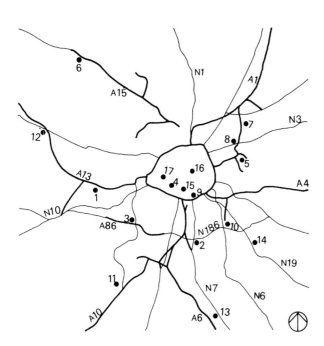

2.22 Paris region: plan showing new shopping centres
built during the suburban expansion of the 1970s.
Key: (1) Parly 2 (completed 1969); (2) Belle Epine
(1971); (3) Velizy 2 (1972); (4) Maine-Montparnasse
(1973); (5) Rosny 2 (1973); (6) 3 Fontaines (1973);
(7) Pavinor (1974); (8) Bobigny 2 (1974);
(9) Massena 13 (1974); (10) Creteil Soleil (1974);
(11) Ulis 2 (1974); (12) Art de Vivre (1975);
(13) Evry 2 (1975); (14) Boissy 2 (1976);
(15) Galaxie (1976); (16) Le Forum des Halles
(1979); (17) Beau Grenelle (1979).

form without taking account of this external
context. By contrast the North American centres,
hermetically sealed within their asphalt perimeters,
were free to evolve solutions determined purely by
the internal functional brief. Under pressure of
competition and with more prosperous catchment
areas, they adopted the enclosed mall more rapidly
than in Europe, and by the mid 1960s were able to
show a profusion of standard models which had a
profound impact on visiting European developers,
architects and agents. Thus, in 1969 (*Shopping for
Pleasure*: 7) we have:

Sometimes one hears that North American experience can
have little relevance to the UK situation. Whatever the
initial doubts the visiting party may have had as to the
value of this study, these were quickly dispelled. We were
soon convinced that there was much to learn from both
USA and Canadian experience which could be employed in
the UK.

and in 1970 (L. Marler in *Design for Shopping*: 5):

In North America over one-third of retail trade was done
in shopping centres as long ago as 1966. By the end of this
year the figure will be approaching one-half, with nearly
200 million square feet of shopping space, mostly
air-conditioned, being added each year. We may not
advance with this speed in Britain, but one thing is certain;
once the housewife and retailer have discovered the
comfort and efficiency of modern shopping-centre
shopping they will become increasingly disenchanted with
anything else.

and again in 1972 (Chapman, R. G., Carran, R.
and Mills, P., *Shopping Around*: 1–12):

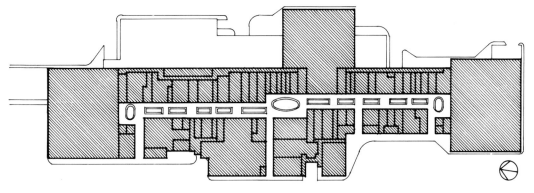

2.23 Rosny 2, Paris: plan of upper mall level. 1 : 3,000.

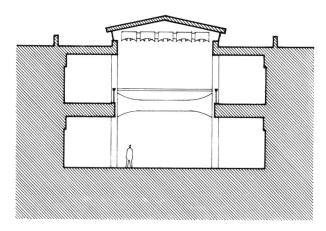

2.24 Parly 2, Paris: section through main mall. 1 : 300.

Our purpose was to learn from the vast experience of shopping centres in North America and to see how these lessons could be applied to British situations. . . . In effect . . . we are in the fortunate position of being able to look into a crystal ball and catch a glimpse of how UK shopping could develop.

The influence of American models was nowhere more marked than in France, which had entered the field of post-war retail construction later than the northern European countries. By the late 1960s Paris was in the process of being equipped with a dozen large centres based closely on the American pattern, and adopting strategic positions on the burgeoning *autoroute* network of the region. They included the '2' series built by the Société des Centres Commerciaux, as well as other similar new town centres which accompanied the rapid expansion of suburban development around the city [2.22]. Many of these projects were carried out by consultants with American experience, and most notably Larry Smith Consulting as real estate consultants, and Lathrop Douglass-Aaron Chelouche SARL as architects. The plan form adopted was commonly that of the simple dumb-bell arrangement, with two mall levels served by flanking car parks, often decked to achieve sufficient parking numbers on more limited sites than in North America. Thus at Parly 2 five major stores (SUM, Printemps, BHV and Prisunic department stores and Drugwest) were clustered at each end of the straight, 200-metre-long mall space. In subsequent examples the mall length was extended to 250 metres (Velizy 2), and 280 metres (Rosny 2) and secondary magnets introduced to reinforce the central zone, sometimes, as at Rosny 2 [2.23], with a shift in mall alignment at this point to reduce the visual length of the scheme.

The mall section was similarly standardised, with a double-height central zone bridged at intervals by the upper level deck [2.24]. And along with these organisational patterns, the French centres adapted the characteristic iconography of the American product, from the signs and flag-poles identifying the site from the highway, through the entry features which punctuate the blank exterior of the introverted centre [2.25], into the malls themselves, with their low artificial lighting levels and profusion of finishes and suspended ceiling patterns – glittery and exciting or brittle and garish according to taste – and concluding at squares fitted out with planting, glycerine fountains and promotional booths [2.26]. Mall cafes, taking the place of the American fast-food operations, and the occasional specialty area, as where a section of lower mall lined with food shops might be paved in brick to indicate the atmosphere of a street market, completed the formula.

In the UK a different set of circumstances, in particular as regards planning controls on out-of-town developments, effectively prevented such a wholesale and literal transposition of the American model. However, the combination of enclosed mall and glitter was introduced during the 1960s in the series of Arndale shopping centres, smaller than the French examples, and built in a number of towns in England by the developer Sam Chippendale. In terms of character and scale, as well as mall plan and sectional organisation, the closest English comparisons to the continental centres were provided by the Victoria Centre in

19

2.25 Creteil Soleil, Paris: view of entrance from car
park.

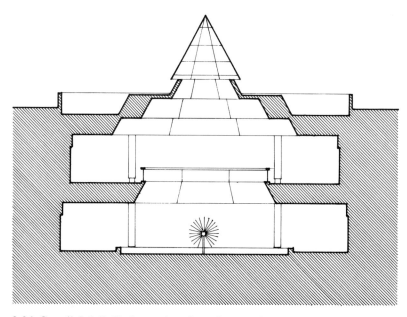

2.26 Creteil Soleil, Paris: section through central square.
1 : 300.

Nottingham and Brent Cross in London. In the former case, completed in 1972, the restricted urban site, formerly occupied by a railway terminus, resulted in the sandwiching of a two-storey, 200-metre dumb-bell mall between layers of car parking below and housing above [2.27]. Four years later, after a protracted period for planning approval, Brent Cross, the first and only out-of-town regional centre to be built on the American and French pattern in the UK, was opened at a strategic location on the North Circular Road. Using the customary split-level site section of those models to bring a balanced flow of shoppers down

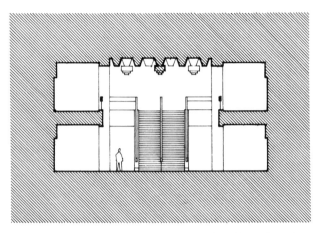

2.27 Victoria Centre, Nottingham: section through main mall. 1 : 300.

side malls into the two sales levels, the main mall again runs for 200 metres between end magnet department stores. Its alignment is staggered at a central square, as at Rosny 2, although its treatment is more sober than the tinselled French malls, with baffled roof-top natural lighting introduced along the length of the main mall [2.28]. Externally [2.29] the monumental scale of the department store entrances is more reminiscent of American centres in which the assertion of an up-market quality and a semi-independent status within the overall development is a characteristic feature of their external treatment.

Indeed the key role played by the department store in American regional centres, both in letting and financial terms and also in setting the standards for the treatment of the rest of the scheme, was a crucial factor in the development of their mall, as well as exterior, form. And just as the department store had undergone a gradual transformation from its earliest nineteenth-century origins as a low-cost, high-turnover trading operation (reflected in its Continental names, 'Bon Marché' – 'cheap', and 'Warenhaus' – 'warehouse') into its present high-service, high-quality form, so also the large American centres moved progressively up-market in their search for competitive advantage in terms of amenity rather than cost. Thus, by the time these European versions of the independent enclosed shopping centre were on the ground, the Americans had already moved on to the third, and probably final, stage of its development.

2.28 Brent Cross, London: view of main mall.

2.29 Brent Cross, London: view of department store
exterior.

Chapter 3 The department store mall

It had been early recognised that the very notion of a purpose-built shopping centre was analogous to that of a department store (Gruen and Smith 1960:80):

It has often been said that a shopping center is actually a department store in which various departments are placed in separate buildings. The truth of this statement, even though it is an over simplification, becomes even more apparent in centers with covered pedestrian areas because of their resemblance to early department stores built round a well [*3.1*].

The enclosure of the mall was a crucial step in turning the analogy into a physical fact. At that point it became necessary to relate structure, finishes, environmental systems and activities between public and private areas. But although a degree of physical integration was thus achieved, there is a sense in which the notion of the mall as a department store was not yet, in the centres of the 1960s, a psychological fact. The mall was still a parallel-sided, arcaded street, and although the glass windows might be removed from the shop-fronts and floor finishes carried across the threshold, the line of demarcation between public discipline and private display remained.

By abandoning the maximum visibility rule, which had produced the regular mall alignments of that period, the new centres of the 1970s overcame that implicit difference of style between landlord and tenant areas. Released from that constraint, the character of the mall now underwent a new transformation. In terms of plan form and basic organisational patterns these centres broke little new ground, and indeed the features of mall design were almost all present in earlier schemes. But by developing and intensifying these themes they created a new kind of synthesis of the shopping centre components in which the mall, now labyrinthine and complex, now monumental and vast, acted as the core organising element of a single 'department' centre.

3.1 Bon Marché department store, Paris: cast-iron and
glass interior of store designed by Eiffel and
Boileau, 1876.

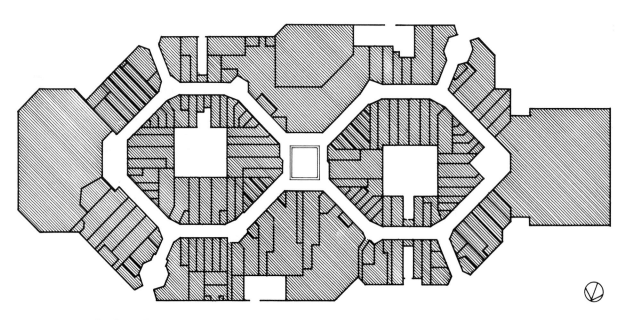

3.2 Sherway Gardens, Toronto: plan. 1 : 3,000.

3.3 Sherway Gardens, Toronto: view of small square.

3.4 Sherway Gardens, Toronto: view of central square.

One of the first projects to explore the possibilities of a more elaborate mall geometry was Sherway Gardens on the west side of Toronto. Its three major mall squares are disposed regularly down the long axis of a standard two-magnet development [3.2], but instead of being connected by straightforward orthogonal routes, the malls adopt a meandering alignment, forming an 'S' configuration in the first, 1971, phase, and later developing into a full figure-of-eight plan with the completion of the centre in 1975. At each change of direction in the hexagonal mall geometry a pool of natural light picks out some identifying characteristic of the smaller squares formed at these points, as 'Desert Garden', 'Aquarium Garden', 'Japanese Garden', 'Clock Court', and so on [3.3]. The two larger courts at each end of the circuit act as ante-rooms to the department stores, Simpson's and Eaton's, and at the centre of the plan the largest public space, Sherway Square, is set out as a formal architectural set piece, with powerful egg-crate roof structure, to accommodate exhibitions, performances and events [3.4]. The malls thus provide a carefully modulated sequence of conditions, from the short entrance side malls, through the range of intermediate spaces, to the strongly articulated central place. This spatial sequence provides a corresponding range of conditions for the letting pattern, from service functions, such as banks, hairdressers and post office, on the side-mall frontages, through standard units on the main malls, more intensive clusters of small units around courts, the Gourmet Fair with some thirty-eight different food and drink concessions beside the central square, to the department stores themselves.

The varied functional uses of the centre are thus orchestrated by the carefully controlled mall sequence, and this integration is a feature of this third stage of development of the out-of-town centres. At Sherway Gardens the ingenious plan form was particularly effective, not only in allowing a simple means of phasing the development, but also in providing a large amount of single-level shopping with prime mall frontage, through the creation of a circuit, rather than a linear, route. For the majority of the larger centres a two-level mall arrangement served the same purpose, and did not require the invention of such unconventional plan forms. However, the principles of compression and elaboration were similarly applied to achieve dramatic and highly orchestrated versions of familiar organisational types.

Opened in the same year as Sherway Gardens, Woodfield Mall at Schaumburg, north-west of Chicago, was a very large regional centre indeed,

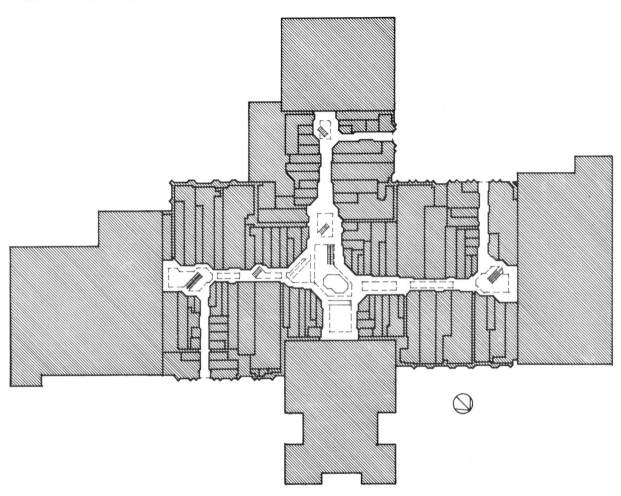

3.5   Woodfield Mall, Schaumburg, Illinois: plan of lower
       mall level. 1 : 3,000.

providing some 190,000 sq. metres of gross leasable
area (GLA). Despite this, the designers were able
to establish shorter magnet intervals than at
Yorkdale, for example, in a 'T' plan with four
magnet stores, in which one of the stores is located
close to the central crossing-point. This was
achieved by the use of multiple levels and by
expanding the width of the centre by some 50 per
cent over the Yorkdale case [3.5]. The resulting
intensification of activity along the main mall
frontages is further increased by inserting a third,
mezzanine, level at two opposite corners of the
central square. Far from the simple cross-wall
arrangements of earlier schemes, where shops
occupy what appear in effect as the regular
subdivisions of an urban plot, the letting plan at
Woodfield Mall comprises a complex assembling of
large and small units, packed together in plan and
section to fill the available volume. Indeed it is as
if the overall building block has been carved and
split and excavated to achieve the maximum
frontage use, and this analogy is carried over into
the treatment of the mall itself, whose vertical and
horizontal profiles broaden and narrow like a
system of caverns tunnelled through the internal
strata.

As at Sherway Gardens, the sequence of
movement through these caverns is carefully
controlled, and highly theatrical. It consists of two
stages, the first isolating the outside world and
introducing the internal organisation, and the
second repeating the progression of the first but at
a larger and more dramatic scale. Leaving the
comfort of her air-conditioned car, the shopper
hurries across the sun-broiled or rain-swept tarmac
and thankfully passes through doors into an air-
conditioned side mall. Drawn down this relatively
dark, single-level tunnel, lined with secondary
units, by the pool of light ahead, she reaches one
of the squares located at the end of each arm of
the main mall system. She discovers this to be a
two-storey space, which she has entered at either
upper or lower level, according to the direction
of approach. On one side of the cavern is a magnet
department store, but before deciding to enter it
she turns to see that a second tunnel [3.6; 3.7],
much taller than the first and with natural light
spilling through holes punched in its roof, leads off
into the heart of the building. Following this route,
past the undulating frontages of standard units, the
tunnel gradually widens as it approaches a second
cavern, again much larger than the first. As she

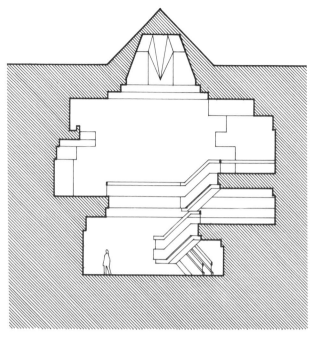

3.6   Woodfield Mall, Schaumburg, Illinois: view of main mall.

3.7   Woodfield Mall, Schaumburg, Illinois: section through main mall. 1: 300

3.8   Woodfield Mall, Schaumburg, Illinois: view of central square.

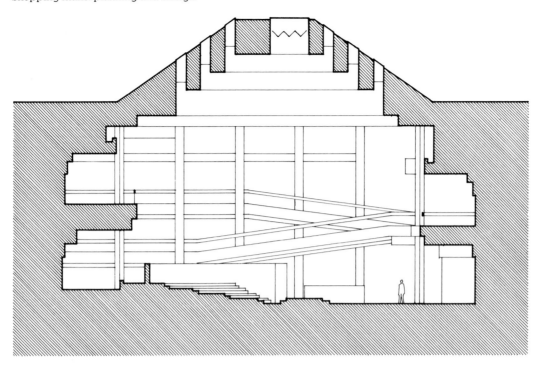

3.9 Woodfield Mall, Schaumburg, Illinois: section
through central square. 1 : 300.

3.10 Woodfield Mall, Schaumburg, Illinois: view from car
park of perimeter servicing bay.

draws closer, the gallery floor on one side of the tunnel splits up and down to create the intermediate mezzanine level, and shop frontages become more closely packed. The route now culminates in the central space, Grand Court [*3.8*], into which light filters from slots carved into the layers of its ceiling rising overhead [*3.9*]. Its floor too has been quarried and shaped to form an amphitheatre and pools, while all round its perimeter the incoming galleries at their various levels are linked by bridging ramps and stairs.

The geological evocation of this centre is echoed in a number of those which followed and is consistent with the emphasis upon the creation of a plausible internal, even subterranean world, full of visual interest and variety, in which one is tempted, not simply to pass through, but to stay. The element of fantasy is implied, but never made quite explicit. One would, after all, despite the grotto-like character of the interior, be mildly surprised to see the seven dwarfs come marching down the ramps of Woodfield Mall and set to work on the glittering crystalline stalagmites which sprout from the cavern floor. Yet the implicit reference to an Aladdin's cave for Gucci-clad suburban miners is difficult to avoid altogether.

In pursuit of the magical central space, designers simplified and suppressed features of earlier schemes which elaborated other aspects of their function and cost money. Thus trucking tunnels, which provided basement service access to stores out of sight of the incoming shoppers, were generally abandoned as an over-sophistication. Instead the smallest possible truck bays were cut into the blank fortress-like exterior walls, with vehicles (and armed security guards) queuing in the car park [*3.10*], and some hand-trucking to small central units accepted. As one designer put it, 'If someone's doing good business they'll get their product in somehow.' Instead resources were concentrated 'up front', in the mall, and in particular in the central space.

This emphasis is apparent at the Eastridge Center at San Jose in California, in which a plan form and use of inserted mezzanines very similar to those of Woodfield Mall were employed. Here the central space sprawls right across the middle of the plan [*3.11*], between the two department stores located on the shorter axis. With more subdued roof lighting than at Woodfield, the faceted galleries surround a huge area, some 100 metres long [*3.12*]. At Santa Anita Fashion Park in Los Angeles the cathedral-like scale of the central place is further emphasised by two rows of monumental cylindrical columns which rise through the space [*3.13*; *3.14*]. Of the $70 million spent on this project, opened in 1974, some $200,000 was devoted to a collection of 'sculpture and artefacts'

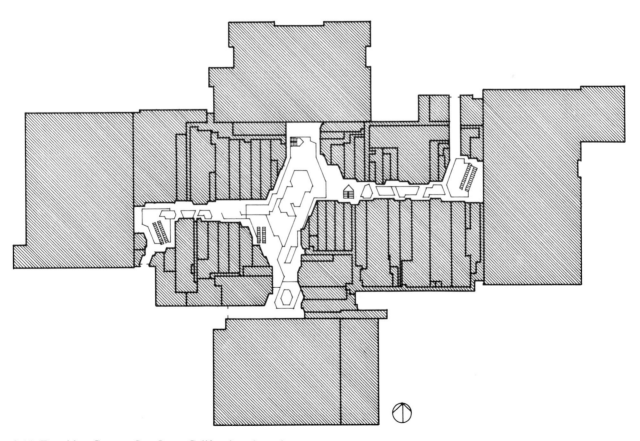

3.11 Eastridge Center, San Jose, California: plan of lower mall level. 1 : 3,000.

3.12 Eastridge Center, San Jose, California: view of central square.

installed in the mall, and including, in the central space, the largest sculpture to be created by Roy Lichtenstein, formed in timber with a brilliant blue plastic skin, and a full-sized replica of the Wright Brothers' 'Flyer' biplane, which soars above the wooded garden and childrens' crèche formed in the floor of the central nave.

The devotion of large sums of money to conspicuous art works, indicative, along with the lavish scale of the public spaces, of the quality of the centre, is a common theme. At Northbrook Court, outside Chicago, the mall is punctuated by four squares [3.15; 3.16], each tailored around a central top-lit, free-standing structure which supports a specially commissioned 10-metre-high steel sculpture [3.17]. Designed and fabricated by the sculptor Charles O. Perry in Rome, they were shipped to Northbrook where:

They don't flash or clash or make cute noises. They're just very handsome, and that's just right for Northbrook Court.

(Northbrook Court publicity)

The surrounding building reinforces this expectation:

Our interior walls are covered with a million pounds of the finest travertine. Our floors are parquet because it's quiet and very nice to walk on. There are upholstered couches to rest on and if you're lucky you might get to see a Balanchine ballet at the Court on a soft summer afternoon.

(op. cit.)

And the products sold in the adjoining shops confirm it:

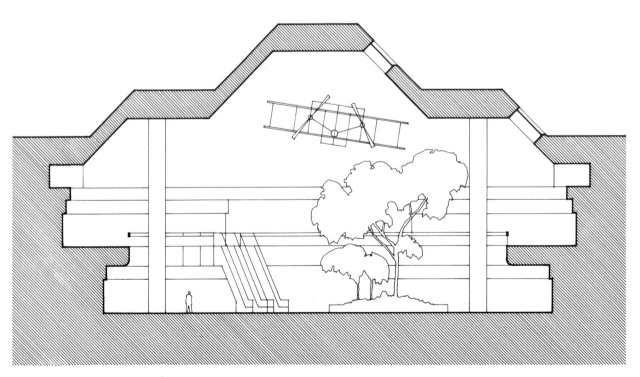

3.13 Santa Anita Fashion Park, Los Angeles: section through central square. 1 : 300.

3.14 Santa Anita Fashion Park, Los Angeles: view of
central square.

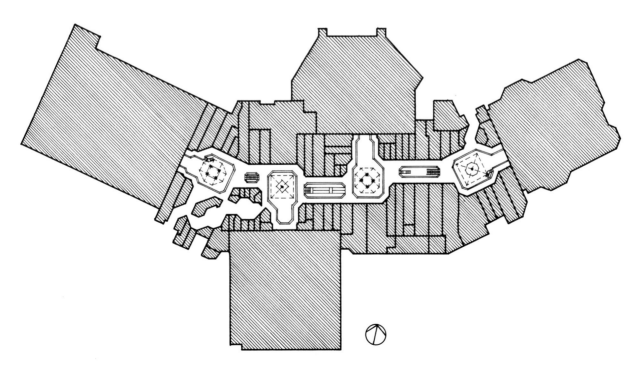

3.15 Northbrook Court, Northbrook, Illinois: plan of
upper mall level. 1 : 3,000.

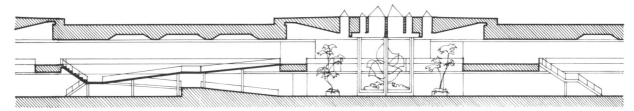

3.16 Northbrook Court, Northbrook, Illinois: section
along central mall. 1 : 600.

3.17 Northbrook Court, Northbrook, Illinois: view of
one of the four 'sculpture courts'.

For the person who has everything!! Now there's
'sculptaire': only at Barrett!! What is sculptaire you ask?
It's a natural diamond that has been cut and fashioned into
gems of unusual and intriguing designs. Square cut or pear
shaped they are not!! At present, Barrett Jewelers has a
limited number of butterflies, horseheads, trees, fish and
stars!! No two stones are exactly alike nor are the prices,
from $1,500 to $11,000!!

(Northbrook Court Merchants' Newsheet *The Court
Report*, July 1981)

Not all such centres were so insistently up-
market, and the idea of the mall as not simply the
most direct public thoroughfare from magnet to
magnet, but as an ordered network of varied
internal spaces providing a controlling sequence for
both the letting plan and the experience of a

centre, was applied to a wide range of projects. At
Scarborough Town Centre, Toronto, the 1973 first-
stage 'L' plan was enlarged in 1979 to complete a
square two-level mall circuit [*3.18*], with three
department stores and a supermarket at its corners
around which a variety of small and standard units
were tightly packed. Public spaces then ranged
from artificially lit, predominantly single-level
malls, to double-height spaces at the corner
junctions, with natural light introduced through
roof slots and incorporating a few carefully
designed feature elements, such as a glazed wall-
climber lift [*3.19*], and an ingenious cluster of hot-
air balloons which rise and fall on guide wires
powered by warm-air blower nozzles set in a pool
in the mall floor [*3.20*]. Finally the mall expanded
at one corner into a fully roof glazed fast-food area

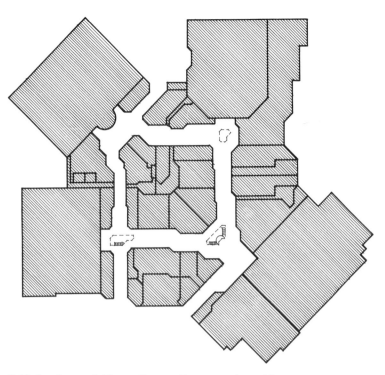

3.18 Scarborough Town Centre, Toronto: plan of lower
      mall level. 1 : 3,000.

3.19 Scarborough Town Centre, Toronto: view of free-
      standing wall-climber lift in one corner square.

3.20 Scarborough Town Centre, Toronto: view of hot-air
      balloons in another square.

[*3.21*], with free-standing brightly coloured space-frame parasol structure and generous planting.

The integral use of planting was indeed a discovery of this period, or at least a development of earlier isolated experiments, which reinforced the softer-sell approach of the mall. The introduction of semi-tropical species, shipped up from special nurseries in Florida, hinted at the slightly exotic character of the mall environment without being overly grandiose. In this respect they provided an ideal device for the upgrading of earlier, open centres laid out on the regimented and now tedious patterns of the maximum visibility rule. Thus, at the Don Mills Centre in Toronto, a 1954 development was successfully refurbished and its mall character brought up to date in 1978 by roofing and repairing the mall, and planting a row of trees down its centre. Besides softening the

earlier, somewhat brittle character, the trees had the effect of screening the length of a 10-metre-wide, 250-metre-long and relentlessly straight mall [*3.22; 3.23*], so that, as with the undulating plan forms of later schemes, it is only revealed in short lengths.

But the full possibilities of the mall as the central, dramatic space of an integrated 'department' centre are only revealed in the largest regional centres of this period, and it is perhaps appropriate to conclude with an example designed by the firm which began the process at Southdale, Minneapolis, and which they consider to be among their most successful.

The site for Fox Hills Mall was a difficult one. Small, at 20 hectares, for a 100,000-sq. metre centre with surface parking, it was traversed by the high-level Marina Freeway in western Los Angeles,

3.21 Scarborough Town Centre, Toronto: fast-food area off the main mall circuit.

3.22 Don Mills Centre, Toronto: view down refurbished
    mall.

3.23 Don Mills Centre, Toronto: view of refurbished
    square formed at mall junction.

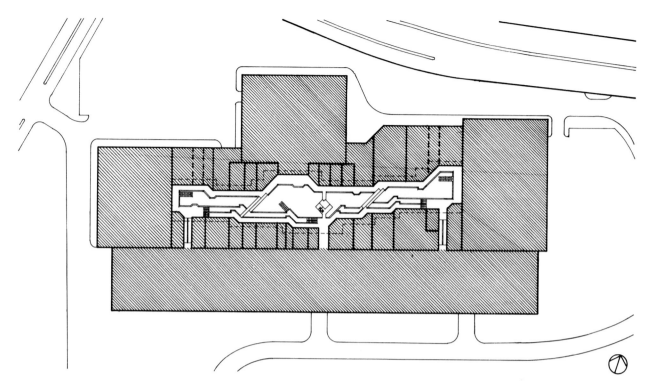

3.24 Fox Hills Mall, Los Angeles: plan of upper mall
level. 1 : 3,000.

and peppered with oil wells [3.24]. To achieve
sufficient car parking, Gruen Associates were
obliged to incorporate a decked parking solution,
and this took the form of a 360-metre long,
four/five storey split-level parking structure pushed
against the southern boundary of the site and
forming the south wall of a linear, three-magnet
centre. The parking decks were then used to feed
directly into three shopping levels on the south side
of the east–west running mall, with two levels built
on its north side. Department stores were located
at each end and in the middle of the north side.

In this scheme the distinction between mall and
square, which began to be eroded at Woodfield and
Eastridge with the sprawling expansion of the
central court, finally disappears. The public space
forms a continuous valley or canyon carved down
the length of the centre [3.25], 250 metres long
between department stores and varying in width
between 22 and 42 metres. Overhead, flank walls
are extended up from the valley sides and stagger
back and forward on plan as the valley meanders
down the block. These walls carry roof units
spanning the space, and allowing natural light to
enter through slots between them and reflect along
their curved soffits. The units are set at varying
heights to form an undulating profile, rising at the
middle and each end to correspond to a widening
of the mall space at these, the vestigial square
positions. The valley is thus modulated in plan and
section to acknowledge variations in activity along
its length, and in addition is crossed by ramped

bridges linking the offset gallery levels on each side
[3.26]. In the middle a steel stair structure, like a
giant climbing frame, links all the levels, and
escalators dive down among the pools on the valley
floor. The spatial gymnastics which are thus built
around a simple, unified mall organisation create a
highly varied and eventful place, a true adventure
playground for adults.

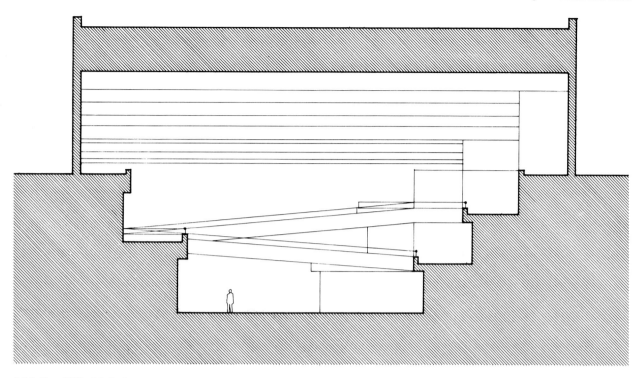

3.25 Fox Hills Mall, Los Angeles: section through mall.
1 : 300.

3.26 Fox Hills Mall, Los Angeles: view down central
'valley' mall.

Chapter 4 The return of the arcade

The dramatic rise of energy costs in 1973 and succeeding years introduced a new critical element in the appraisal of successful building design, and one which, in the case of shopping centres at least, had clear implications. In an analysis of energy usage in a typical American centre it was found that some 70 per cent of all energy consumed was attributable to artificial lighting, with heating, ventilation and air conditioning accounting for 28 per cent and miscellaneous items such as lifts and escalators the remaining 2 per cent.[1] Moreover, a substantial proportion of the air-conditioning load was itself required to remove excess heat resulting from lighting. Thus the substitution of natural for artificial lighting in a centre, most readily achieved in the mall areas, would have substantial benefits in terms of energy usage. 'Elements designed to maximise use of daylight, such as atriums or courts which are designed with a capability of redirecting light, produce results (40% reduction in yearly lighting power demand).' (Dahl 1980)

This appreciation was adopted in energy-conserving legislation in most states of the USA, limiting the artificial lighting output per square metre in shopping centres, but, as often happens, fashion had anticipated these functional criteria, and several years before the energy crisis, mall designs were appearing in which natural lighting played a new and significant role.

The splayed roof profile of the main space of Santa Anita Fashion Park recalls an earlier design for the project in which Cesar Pelli proposed a novel mall in the form of a linear arcade spine, asymmetrical in section and glazed along its tilted, southern side [4.1]. This interpretation of the mall, not as a free-form space carved out of a retail block, but as a regular, identifiable element, of clear axial rectitude and independent structure and form, was described by Pelli as 'a modern main

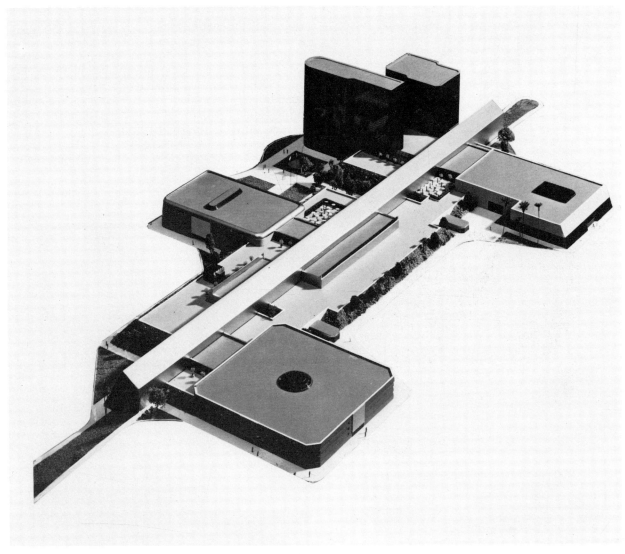

4.1 Santa Anita Fashion Park, Los Angeles: early study
by Cesar Pelli.

street – multi-levelled and air conditioned'.[2] With
its continuously glazed profile, scooping sunlight
into its section, it suggested a mall character – tall,
light, airy and linear – in contrast to the user
spaces it served, and one which recalled earlier
models of arcaded streets.

Though the project was never built in this form,
Pelli went on to design a small shopping mall at The
Commons in Columbus, Indiana, in 1973, which
incorporated a totally glazed double-pitched roof
[4.2], as part of a sequence of steel-framed,
naturally lit, geometric public spaces [4.3; 4.4]. This
was followed by two buildings, the Winter Garden
at Niagara Falls [4.5], and the Pacific Design
Center in Los Angeles [4.6], in which Pelli was
able to create glazed spaces comparable in scale to
the Santa Anita project. In the second of these,
opened in 1976 and housing 70,000 sq. metres of
showroom and exhibition space for the interior
design industry, it is as if the sleek extruded mall
of Santa Anita had expanded to absorb its flanking

user spaces. Clad in blue opaque insulated glass,
the 'Blue Whale' was crowned by a barrel vault,
bronze-glazed on one side, which runs down its
170-metre length, and again scoops light down into
a 'Grand Court' which forms the focus of its upper
floors.

If this succession of projects suggested a
preference for an alternative view of the nature of
the public mall from that of an essentially artificial
department store space writ large, and one which
predated the economic argument for more
extensive natural lighting, it was not unique in this.
With its simple linear geometry, huge glazed roof
vault, and explicit reference to a nineteenth-century
model (the Galleria Vittorio Emanuele II in
Milan), the Galleria at Post Oak on the Houston
loop similarly rejected the subterranean grotto
character pursued elsewhere. In the first phase of
this development, completed in 1970, three mall
levels, fed by multi-storey parking decks outside,
form galleries around the large central space,

covered by the continuous glazed vault, 12 metres wide and 168 metres long [*4.7*], [*4.8*]. At the lowest level this space is occupied, not by planters, sculpture, fountains and trees, but by a sheet of ice, an element as exotic and compelling in the hot and humid Houston climate (where the air-conditioned Astrodome is not a luxury for playing professional football, but a necessity) as a tropical garden would be in a northern city.

If it is then possible to see in these American projects of the early 1970s a rather different mall character from that described in Chapter 3, it is

4.2   The Commons, Columbus, Indiana: view of shopping mall.

4.3   The Commons, Columbus, Indiana: circular stall units in the main hall.

4.4   The Commons, Columbus, Indiana: view of main hall.

4.5 The Winter Garden, Niagara Falls, N.Y.: view of interior.

4.6 The Pacific Design Center, Los Angeles: view of upper level of Grand Court.

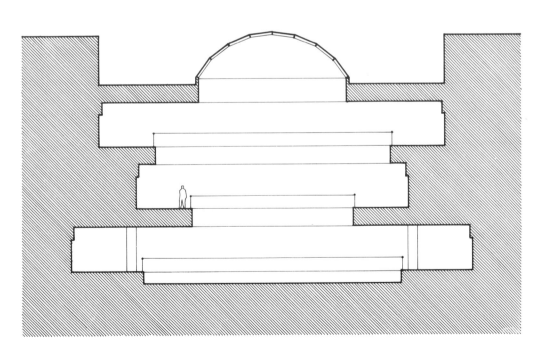

4.7 The Galleria, Houston: section through central space of first phase. 1 : 300.

also important to recognise that the difference is more than one of a certain preference for roof glazing. The sequence which led from Southdale to Parly 2, and then on to Woodfield Mall, Eastridge and Fox Hills, saw the principal challenge in mall design as that of unifying the internal planning components of the shopping centre in a single modulated enterprise, in which the public space was essentially, as Gruen had described, the central well of a gigantic department store. This unification implied the blurring of the mall/shop boundary, the treatment of mall detailing as shopfitting, and, above all, the internalisation of the mall, as a space quite distinct from the public area which lay beyond the entrance doors. In these terms Pelli's Santa Anita mall, an open-ended axis slicing through the development, is quite inappropriate, for it stubbornly insists on asserting its separate identity as a street, and in maintaining contact with the outside throughout its length. Whether for reasons of boredom with the trenchant artificiality of the department store mall, or unease at its emphatic rejection of the world outside, such schemes began to detach the public spaces from

their immediate context, to restore their integrity in plan and section with clearly defined forms and architectonic detailing, and to suggest the possibility of their reference to events beyond the hermetic capsule of the shopping centre. Inevitably perhaps, they thus called up the images of earlier urban models – the street, the arcade and the gallery.

A similar line of investigation can be found in Europe. Already in 1966 the Rodovre Centrum outside Copenhagen had suggested a very different quality of interior space from that created in the contemporary English Arndale Centres, or later French projects, both of which closely followed the American mainstream developments. With laminated timber roof beams carrying continuous glass and plastic translucent roof sheeting, and themselves supported on a simple exposed steel frame, the malls were light and unassertively elegant [4.9]. This atmosphere was further reinforced by the ability of some roof sections to roll back to open up the squares in summer, and by one of the most ambitious interior planting schemes of its period, appropriately enough, since the developer, A. Knudsen, had formerly had a market garden on the site.

Closer to the studies of mall form carried out by Cesar Pelli, a number of projects by James Stirling and Michael Wilford in the 1960s and early 1970s show a similar interest in the arcaded route as a distinctive public space in contrast to the solid user volumes it serves. Beginning modestly as a glazed bridge or link, as at Queen's College, Oxford, in 1966 [4.10], or promenade deck as at St Andrew's University and the Runcorn housing [4.11], the element blossomed into a fully articulated space at the Olivetti Training School at Haslemere [4.12], and in the linear concourse for the Olivetti headquarters project at Milton Keynes [4.13]. Finally, in the Derby Civic Centre competition entry of 1970, a project on which Leon Krier worked while in Stirling's office, the arcaded route was applied to the problem of a shopping street in a city centre, and in a form, with symmetrical tall barrel-vaulted section [4.14], which for the first time in Stirling's work clearly recalls the nineteenth-century precedent. With its heavy arched structural members, the design is also reminiscent of the 1965 project by O. M. Ungers [4.15], for the Tiergarten Museum in Berlin in which a similarly profiled element was used to define a public route through the building.

Whatever the intention of historical references in the use of this form, its distinctive self-contained geometry, adaptable to a range of linear mall spans, and clearly distinguishable from the rectangular framed user volumes it accompanied, made it an ideal device for establishing an identifiable route element in a building complex. Implying a defined space along the length below the vault, and signifying 'entry' where it emerged at the building perimeter, the curved vault was thus explicit as a cipher for its function, as Pelli

4.8   The Galleria, Houston: view of interior of first phase, with three shopping levels overlooking the central ice-rink.

4.9   Rodovre Centrum, Copenhagen: view of interior
       mall.

4.10 Queen's College, Oxford: glazed route at upper
      level. (Photographer: Brecht-Einzig Ltd, reproduced
      by courtesy of James Stirling and Michael Wilford)

4.11 Southgate Housing, Runcorn: architect's drawing of access deck. (Courtesy James Stirling and Michael Wilford)

4.12 Olivetti Training School, Haslemere: glazed circulation link. (Photographer: Brecht-Einzig Ltd, reproduced by courtesy of James Stirling and Michael Wilford)

4.13 Olivetti headquarters, Milton Keynes: architect's drawing of central route. (Courtesy James Stirling and Michael Wilford)

demonstrated in his change from the angular mall section of the Santa Anita project to the circular profile at the Pacific Design Center, where the only exterior curved elements, the roof vault and stair tower, signify circulation spaces.

So accessible was the form indeed that it made its appearance in a considerable number of subsequent mall projects, and to such an extent that it was soon in danger of becoming an architectural cliché. However, within the basic geometric configuration, a considerable variety of design solutions was possible for the principal constructional elements of primary structure, glazing support structure, and glazing, the resolution of which constituted a specific architectural vocabulary for the public spaces, just as it had done for the earlier Victorian arcades.

In the Houston Galleria, for example, aluminium I-section bars combined the functions of primary and secondary structure to form a simple faceted vault, with horizontal transom members at each change of plane of the eight-segment span. A similar solution occurred in the Brunel Plaza, the main space of the first phase of the Brunel Centre at Swindon [4.16], but in this case with continuously curved I-sections at 1.2-metre centres, carrying plastic sheet glazing, and hipped rather

4.14 Civic Centre, Derby: architect's drawing of shopping arcade. (Courtesy James Stirling and Michael Wilford)

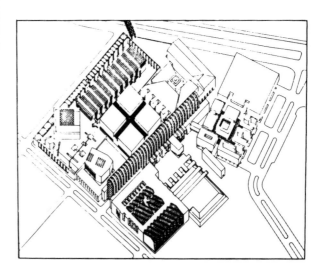

4.15 Project by O. M. Ungers for a museum in the Tiergarten, Berlin.

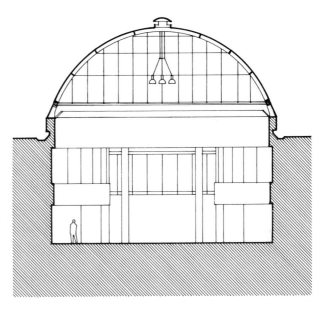

4.16 Brunel Centre, Swindon: section through central square. 1 : 300.

than gable ends. Around the perimeter of this building a continuous canopy was formed with a quarter-circle version of this glazing, but now carried in a powerfully expressed external primary structure, in the form of a steel truss exoskeleton, spanning 24 and 30 metres between column supports [4.17]. In a second phase, the David Murray John Building, tall barrel-vaulted glazed malls [4.18] led to a central space which developed a further and more intricate variant [4.19], with a perforated aluminium I-beam main structure at 5.5 metres, supporting an independent aluminium glazing bar system at 1.1 metres, in turn carrying the curved and tinted plastic glazing sheets. The primary structure was similarly articulated in the

Calwer Strasse Arcade in Stuttgart [4.20], as circular tube sections arched over the space, but this time at the narrower centres of the glazing system held clear on purlin members behind.

Such projects illustrate the possibilities offered by the glazed mall roof structure to develop a vocabulary of public space elements, whether monumental and grand or intimate and complex in scale. They also demonstrate the range of ways in which this structure might engage that of the surrounding development, from the detached solutions of the Houston Galleria and Brunel Plaza, where the canopy floats over the independent tray or frame structure of accommodation below, to the fully engaged design of Stirling's Derby scheme, in

45

4.17 Brunel Centre, Swindon: view of perimeter canopy.

4.18 Brunel Centre, Swindon: view of side mall in David Murray John Building.

4.19 Brunel Centre, Swindon: roof glazing in central square of David Murray John Building.

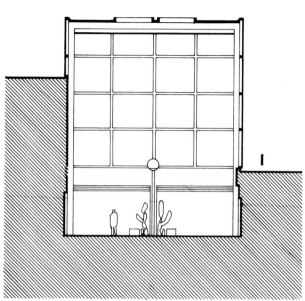

4.20 Calwer Strasse, Stuttgart: section through mall. 1 : 300.

4.21 Milton Keynes Centre: section through main east–west mall. 1 : 300.

which the main building frame rises up to form the primary arch structure of the vault. While the latter achieves a thoroughly integrated treatment of the elements of the space, from floor to ridge, it depends upon the strict control of the adjoining user zones. In practice this was often difficult to achieve, and most solutions adopted a horizontal split of some kind between a lower zone, in which the contingent circumstances of user structure – fire protected, irregularly spaced to suit variable shop widths, and often masked by shop-front conditions – applied, and an upper zone in which the light and regular 'public' structure could run free. The dialogue between these disciplines could then take a variety of forms, as in the David Murray John Building where the primary aluminium roof frame members occurred at the same centres as the concrete columns below, and, though detached from them, developed bracket details which demonstrated the connection between the two systems.

Indeed the way in which the layers met often became a visible explanation of the development circumstances of the building as a whole, and of the relationship between developer and tenant, and hence of public and private space within it. At Milton Keynes, for example, where the development was carried out by a public body, the Milton Keynes Development Corporation, the logic of the mall structure was vigorously enforced through the full height of the mall section [4.21; 4.22], with consequent constraints upon the lettable areas behind. The steel columns of the mall structure rose full height, acting as cross-wall ends to the units and determining a strict 6-metre

4.22 Milton Keynes Centre: view of main east–west mall.

increment of mall frontage. The clarity of the logic of the public space was thus imposed upon the irregular and expedient patterns of private space which usually arise from the negotiations of letting agents and individual tenants for optimum frontage and depth conditions.

If then by 1973, when most of the above examples had been designed, the existence of two general tendencies in mall design, which we may broadly describe as the department store mall and the arcade mall, were already apparent, the effect of the energy crisis was to accentuate the differences of approach which they represented. As energy costs rose, to absorb in some cases 50 per cent of the total running expenses of a centre, so designers seemed faced with divergent strategies for cost-effective environmental design. On the one hand they might consolidate the control of the centre as a single environmental package through more effective hardware; on the other they might reconsider altogether the principle of the fully conditioned, internal mall, and treat the centre as a variable set of circumstances in which the mall might act as a transitional, low-energy space, between exterior and shop.

The former course was adopted in a number of British centres developed on dense urban sites where, as at the Victoria Centre in Nottingham, other uses built on top of the shopping levels tended to impose an upper limit to the mall space. Below this structural constraint a services zone would be established over the mall ceiling, for mall ventilation, smoke extraction and other services, as well as for service feeds to adjoining shop units, and this build-up, strictly limiting the vertical development of the mall space, would then form a major determining feature of the mall character below. In such schemes as the Manchester Arndale Centre, for example, the mall ceiling thus emerged as the single most dominant surface of the public areas [4.23; 4.24]. Unlike the floor, broken up by mall features and the shoppers themselves, and the walls with their variety of shop-fronts, the serviced ceiling, whether modelled or not, imposed itself as a fixed datum.

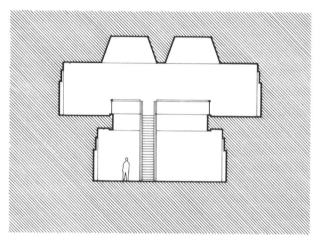

4.23 Arndale Centre, Manchester: section through mall. 1 : 300.

4.24 Arndale Centre, Manchester: view of central square.

4.25 Wood Green Shopping City, London: view of mall.
    (Courtesy Sheppard Robson)

Some of the ways in which such an arrangement could be tuned to minimise energy use were demonstrated at another such centre, Wood Green Shopping City in North London [4.25], in which almost identical design temperatures for public areas and shops (19–21 °C and 20–21 °C respectively) were maintained by a centralised plant room supplying conditioned air to both malls and small units, and hot and chilled water to space users. By the use of a small energy management computer and careful programming of the system to meet the daily patterns of use, it was found possible to reduce gas demand below the minimum originally predicted.[3] In view of the impact of artificial lighting levels on energy costs, those in the mall were reduced as low as 30 lux in general areas, with a reliance on overspill shop-front illumination to enliven the spaces. The contrast between this level and that of natural daylight (the CIE 'standard' sky level is 5,000 lux) further emphasised the internal and artificial character of the public spaces which thus accompanied this approach to their climatic control.

The alternative to this lay in examining the degree to which the mall might operate as a semi-autonomous environment between shop and exterior. At the Irvine Centre in Ayrshire, Scotland, the principle of a services zone extending over both mall and retail areas was retained, but since the main floor was raised above storage levels, without accommodation overhead, natural light was allowed to penetrate into the central mall

through what was, in effect, a structure/services umbrella. This adopted the form of a system of spines and ribs [4.26; 4.27], with the former running the length of the mall, and the latter branching over the sales floors, and together providing a network of roof spaces in which heating and ventilation plant, distribution ducts and pipework, and smoke extract ways could be housed. Glazed clerestory lights were then introduced between the spine and ribs of this steel-framed canopy structure to create naturally lit, though mechanically heated and ventilated, malls. The degree to which these latter systems might be reduced was examined at the Quadrant Centre in Swansea, South Wales, where the developer's initial brief called for a fully air-conditioned mall. As a result of alternative design studies, however, it was decided to eliminate not only cooling but also mechanical ventilation and heating from what were nevertheless intended to be high-quality public spaces. The solution turned on the mall section [4.28], rising through the upper storage floor level and terminating in a pitched roof profile crowned by a ridge element which introduced both natural light and natural ventilation. With more extensive glazed areas in the central square [4.29], and the use of spotlight sources to introduce 'sparkle' in the malls, the public areas thus achieved relative comfort conditions and visual interest with a self-balancing, minimal energy design.

Now if the removal of the fixed ceiling datum and its universal services plenum above freed the designer to investigate more generous mall spaces, it also required a more subtle appreciation of the dynamic factors influencing the mall climate. In effect the Swansea mall section tipped the predominantly horizontal profile of the heavily serviced solution on its side, recalling the vertical proportions of the Victorian arcades. Though widely admired, those models have been hardly examined for their environmental performance,

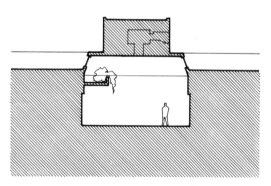

4.26 Irvine Centre, Irvine New Town: section across main mall. 1 : 300.

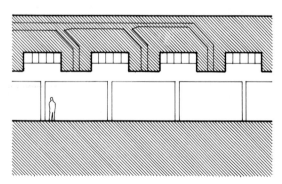

4.27 Irvine Centre, Irvine New Town: section along main mall. 1 : 300.

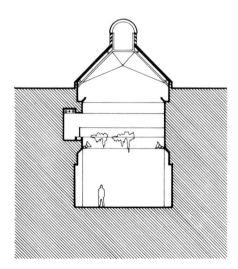

4.28 Quadrant Centre, Swansea: section through mall. 1 : 300.

4.29 Quadrant Centre, Swansea: view of main square.
  (Courtesy Building Design Partnership)

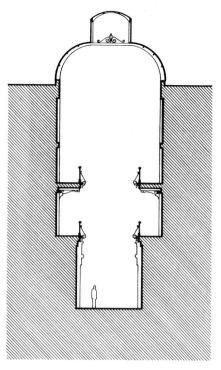

4.30 Barton Arcade, Manchester: section across mall.
1 : 300.

although such observations as have been made suggest their effectiveness in tempering the external climate in both summer and winter. The huge 7.3-hectare enclosure of Paxton's original Crystal Palace was, after all, unheated, though contemporary reports suggest that it was mild and comfortable throughout the winter months, due in part to the heat stored in the ground through the previous summer.[4] Readings taken in a number of simple glazed arcades in Cardiff have shown that, even with open entrances, they are able to maintain a temperature differential of 3 °C or 4 °C with outside conditions in winter, without additional heating.[5]. Similarly, in summer, measurements in Manchester's Barton Arcade indicate no problem of overheating, despite the fully glazed roof [4.30; 4.31]. In the warmer climate of Italy, the Galleria Vittorio Emanuele II serves to illustrate the success of the tall shady arcade section, with ridge venting to induce a natural stack-effect air-flow, in dealing with summer conditions [4.32].

In general these inherent features of the tall glazed mall section have been used in modern projects with some combination of active services systems, particularly for winter heating, and these have provided a further expressive element in the

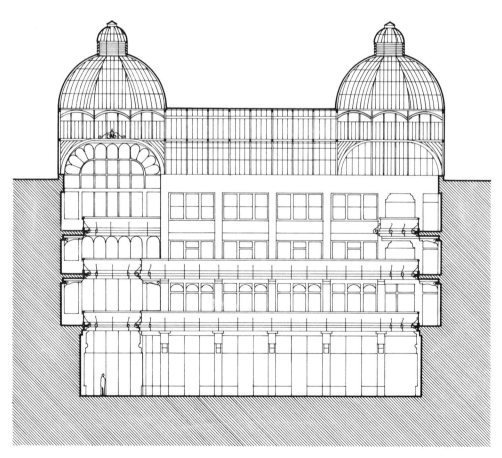

4.31 Barton Arcade, Manchester: section along mall.
1 : 300.

design of such spaces. In the Milton Keynes arcades, despite extensive south-facing upper wall glazing, the stack effect induced by roof vents has been found to be generally successful for summer conditions, boosted if necessary by the mechanical ventilation system. This has output grilles above shop fascias on one side of the mall section and provides winter heating. The unobtrusive character of these services elements, and of their zonal hierarchy, suggests a solution in which the primacy of the structural logic is paramount, and in which a geometrically precise mall system is then equipped with plant to obviate its climatic side-effects. And while this is undoubtedly an over-simplification, it does appear to have been the case that the dynamic characteristics of the latter have required some modification to the envelope, as in the later addition of side mall doors to prevent cross-winds through the orthogonal plan overpowering the entry heater units.[6]

Now just as the resolution of static forces in the structural hierarchy discussed earlier in this chapter may provide a vocabulary for the mall spaces, so also can the manipulation of dynamic environmental factors be made explicit in the hierarchies of services provision which may support the passive characteristics of the tall section. A

simple and graphic illustration of this is provided in the arcade of shops with student rooms overhead which forms the Housing Union Building on the University Campus at Edmonton [4.33], in which the hidden ductwork at Milton Keynes was pulled out into the centre of the space as a free element.

In addition to space heating, cooling and lighting, smoke control forms a further important factor in the design of a space which must form a primary means of escape for shoppers in the event of fire. In the UK the publication from 1970 onwards of research data and design recommendations by the Fire Research Station [7] established a range of measures, including natural or mechanical venting, mall smoke reservoirs of limited length (60 metres) and area (1,000 sq. metres), and smoke curtains and baffles, which themselves constituted a further articulation of the mall space.

The way in which the varied requirements for environmental services might then develop a demonstrative hierarchy within the spatial and structural disciplines of the malls is illustrated by a project for a shopping centre at Waterthorpe, near Sheffield. Low-ceilinged malls provide entry from the perimeter to a central tall-sectional route, formed by steel portal frames bracketed from the edges of the shop ceiling slab [4.35]. Two major nodal spaces articulate changes in direction of the axial route, at which points the standard portals split into half-frames supported in each case by a central free-standing mast structure [4.34]. Clad in solid panels for most of their vertical height, alongside an upper-level service vehicle roadway, the tops of the portals are glazed, while below them the mall section broadens at its base. This reverses the traditional multi-storey Victorian arcade profile, in order to achieve a degree of shading to the artificially lit shop-fronts on each side, and also to provide a location, at the lower angles of the section, for air-handling ducts which

4.32 Galleria Vittorio Emanuele II, Milan: section through mall. 1 : 300.

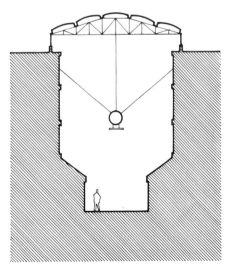

4.33 Housing Union Building, Edmonton: section through mall. 1 : 300.

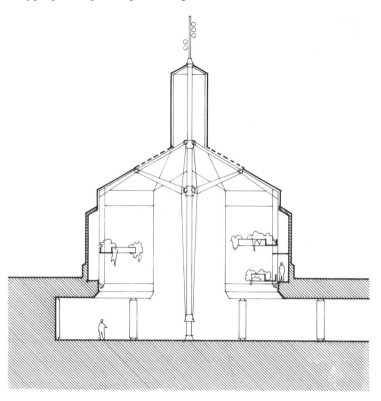

4.34 Waterthorpe Centre, Sheffield: section through square at mall junction. 1 : 300.

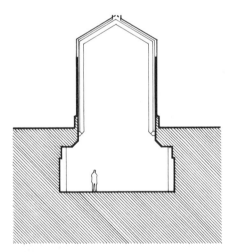

4.35 Waterthorpe Centre, Sheffield: section through typical mall condition. 1 : 300.

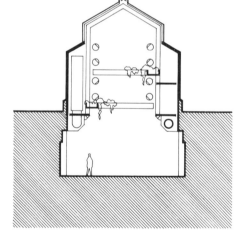

4.36 Waterthorpe Centre, Sheffield: section through mall at main plant locations. 1 : 300.

warm and ventilate the pedestrian concourse. The mechanical plant feeding these continuous duct runs is located in a series of clusters along the length of the mall, at approximately 30-metre intervals, and at these points the solid wall cladding to the upper portal frames detaches itself to form a wider enclosure for the plant units [4.36]. For ease of access, gantry bridges cross at upper level in these positions, and support smoke curtains, planters, special lighting and variable displays, all of which, together with the plant units themselves, can thus be maintained and altered from week to week by

upper level doors from the service road, clear of the mall. In this way the hierarchy of the mechanical services system provides the focus for an intermediate level of visual definition within the malls, between on the one hand the major spatial articulations of the node spaces at 100-metre intervals, and on the other the minor structural rhythm of portal frames and glazing mullions at 3 and 1.5-metre intervals respectively.

In North America the light, arcaded mall was firmly established by the mid 1970s as a generic type, and could be seen in a variety of

4.37 Stanford Mall, Palo Alto, California: view across
main square.

configurations. Where the climate allowed it might
take an entirely open form, as in Palo Alto, south
of San Francisco, where the Stanford Mall created
a series of linked open and roofed spaces [*4.37*],
with a somewhat mannered version of the Brunel
Centre's vaults [*4.38*]. In a series of projects carried
out by the Rouse Company, a less self-conscious,
almost industrial simplicity was applied to the
design of light steel mall canopy structures, clad
with metal decking and glass in a variety of profiles
and supported on free-standing, fire-protected
columns reaching up to the upper shop fascia level.
In the Rouse Company's new town, Columbia, in
Maryland, The Mall in Columbia began this series
with its first phase, opened in 1971 [*4.39; 4.40*].
Hulen Mall at Fort Worth in Texas further
developed it, filling the upper part of the mall
section with its exposed steel truss and space-frame
members [*4.41*], and elaborating the build-up of
glazed areas in the central square [*4.42*]. Again, in
the White Marsh Center in Maryland, the
vocabulary of simple bolted steel angle trusses and
industrial roof sheeting with ridge and eaves glazing
[*4.43*], was accepted as a simple and effective
equivalent of the Victorian cast-iron, patent glazed
arcade, below which the razzmatazz of exposed lift
cages, fountains, shop-fronts and *Ficus benjamina*
might find an appropriate setting.

4.38 Stanford Mall, Palo Alto, California: entrance to
covered square from open mall.

4.39 The Mall in Columbia, Columbia, Maryland: view of mall.

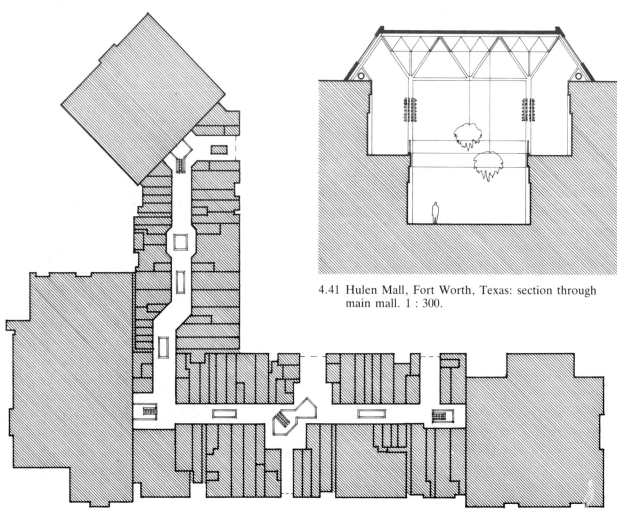

4.41 Hulen Mall, Fort Worth, Texas: section through main mall. 1 : 300.

4.40 The Mall in Columbia, Columbia, Maryland: plan of upper mall level. 1 : 3,000.

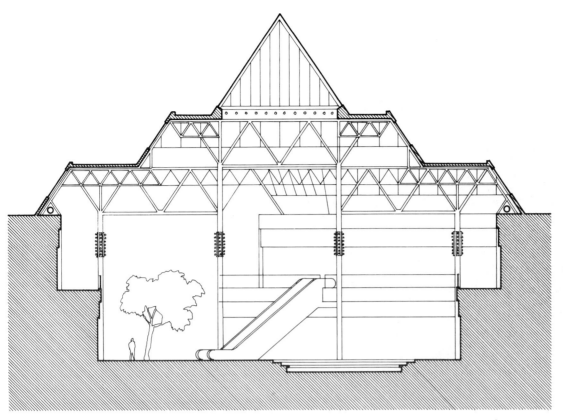

4.42 Hulen Mall, Fort Worth, Texas: section through
central square. 1 : 300.

4.43 White Marsh Center, Maryland: view of central
square.

4.44 The Mall at Chestnut Hill, Boston, Mass.: view of main mall.

A similar, if usually more inflated, approach may be found in a great number of projects of this period carried out by other developers and designers. In the Mall at Chestnut Hill in Boston, for example, a uniform space-frame structure was used across the mall, shaped to follow the variations in the public space below [4.44]. At Oakville Place in Ontario a central 'department store' ceiling was detached from the adjoining user spaces by curved 'arcade' clerestories which developed a second tier in the central space, to build up a Crystal Palace-like profile [4.45].

Unlike most of the British examples, with their preference for single-level malls, these North American projects incorporated the arcaded mall roof over two or more shopping levels, and hence adopted a mall section reducing in width towards the base in a form familiar from Victorian examples such as the Manchester Barton Arcade, where natural roof light was thus brought down to the lowest levels of the section. Since the structure supporting the upper gallery levels was necessarily fire protected, the usual solution was therefore, as we have seen, to treat the architecture of the mall as part of the general building frame until it rose clear of the adjoining shops, and then to cap it with some form of lightweight canopy construction. In another Rouse Company project, in Santa Monica, Los Angeles, Frank Gehry provided an interesting variant on this customary demarcation

4.45 Oakville Place, Ontario: view of main mall.

between user structure and mall structure, by distinguishing the latter, not in its material form, but in the geometry it employed in cutting through the block of retail accommodation. For although the whole building was unified by a common rendered frame and panel treatment of user and mall elements alike, the frame defining the public spaces was set skew within the general grid [4.46], producing a considerable spatial complexity with minimal means [4.47; 4.48], and one which exposed itself in the most dramatic way on the west side of the building, where the skew mall grid burst through the perimeter in an extraordinary construction of frames and terraces facing over the adjoining city blocks towards the beach [4.49].

If it were necessary to select one project which summarises and marks the culmination of the development of the arcade mall type, in the sense that the Eastridge Center or Fox Hills Mall may be said to represent the apotheosis of the department store mall, that project would surely be the Eaton Centre in Toronto. About 20 per cent bigger in each of its dimensions than the Milan Galleria, with a height of 36.5 metres, width of 17 metres and length of 230 metres, the Eaton Centre is essentially a single huge arcade mall space wrapped around with accommodation [4.50; 4.51]. In terms of its structure, services and spatial organisation it illustrates each of the themes explored at a smaller scale in the previous sequence. Underlined by a basement trucking floor, the arcade space rises through three main retail levels, the upper two of which connect with the sloping street outside, and then a further four floors of car parking and offices. This accommodation is supported by 800 mm diameter cylindrical columns, set at about 12-metre centres down the length of the mall, and so

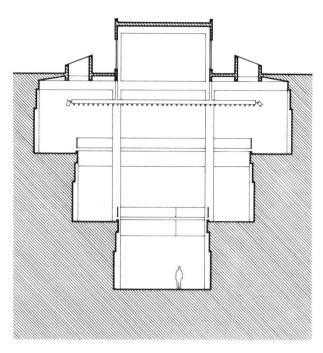

4.47 Santa Monica Place, Los Angeles: section through mall. 1 : 300.

4.48 Santa Monica Place, Los Angeles: view of central square.

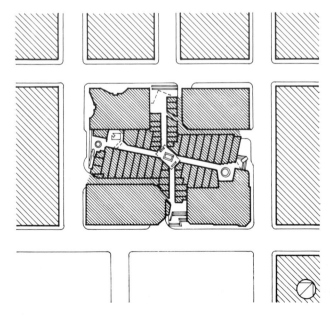

4.46 Santa Monica Place, Los Angeles: ground-floor plan. 1 : 3,000.

4.49 Santa Monica Place, Los Angeles: view of terraces
    on west elevation.

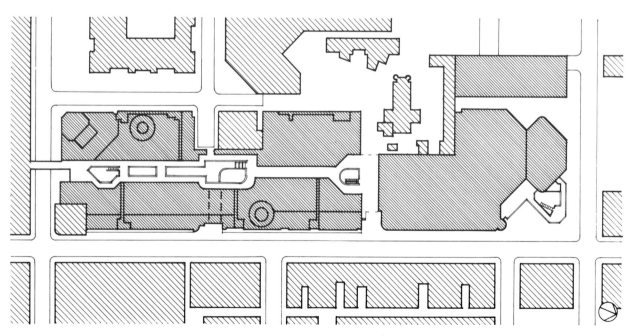

4.50 Eaton Centre, Toronto: plan of upper mall level.
    1 : 3,000.

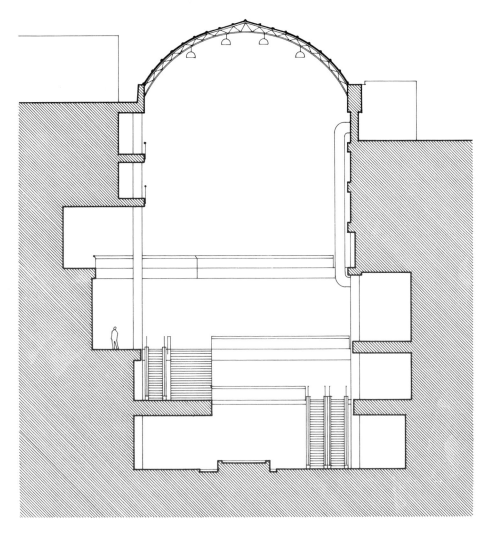

4.51 Eaton Centre, Toronto: section through main mall.
1 : 300.

articulated from infill panels, shop-fronts and floor trays as to preserve the integrity of the giant order they present to the public space [*4.52*]. They terminate in a form of cornice element from which the light roof lattice beams, 400 mm deep and curved to a 9.7-metre radius, spring. These are spaced at 3 metres and in turn carry the roof glazing with mullions at 1-metre intervals along the mall and divided into eighteen panels across the width of the vault [*4.53*].

The environmental control of the huge mall volume is effected in a way similar to that used in the first enclosed centre at Southdale, with heating, ventilating and air-conditioning (HVAC) units at roof level pressurising the mall space, from which shop units draw their air which is then conditioned and recirculated within their zones. Exhaust air is returned to high level from the retail floors by large ducts which climb up the face of the mall walls to discharge through the roof perimeter. The control of smoke in such a large space was hardly envisaged by the existing building codes, and a

first-principles approach, described as the 'Systems Concept to Fire Safe Building Design'[8] was adopted in which a modified version of the normal extract system, with recirculation shut down, would deal with smoke generated within a shop, whereas a fire in the mall itself would send the main HVAC system into reverse, drawing smoke up to high level extract in the mall section.

It is difficult to avoid a comparison between the Eaton Centre and the great Victorian arcades'. The magnetism of its shopping space, coupled with the confident display of its engineering hardware, from its structure and services ductwork to the maintenance gantry which spans below the roof glazing and tracks the length of the mall, all suggest that here the nineteenth-century experiment, abruptly discontinued about 1910, had been restored to a central place in urban development. Yet the period of prosperity and expansion which had produced this result had also given rise to another body of shopping centres in which the whole direction of both arcade and

4.52 Eaton Centre, Toronto: view down central mall,
     looking south.

4.53 Eaton Centre, Toronto: view in central mall.

'department store' complexes was called into doubt, and in which the mall form seemed to revert to an earlier model, of the street as it was imagined to be before the metamorphoses of the Industrial Revolution began.

Notes

1. Study carried out by Gruen Associates and described by William H. Dahl in a paper to International Council of Shopping Centers Conference, Monaco 1981; and in Dahl 1980.

2. Report in *Architectural Record*, Oct. 1970:40.

3. Appraisal in 'Shopping comes in from the cold', *Building Services*, Nov. 1981: 23–6.

4. Green, C. 'The View from the Palace: Joseph Paxton and Large Victorian Greenhouses', unpublished paper, 1982.

5. Study by Sedgwick, P., of BDP Energy Group 1982.

6. For a discussion of the services provision on this project, see Fordham, M. 'Services checkout', *Building Services*, Feb. 1980: 21–5.

7. Summarised in Morgan, H. P., *Smoke Control Methods in Enclosed Shopping Complexes of One or More Storeys: A Design Summary.* HMSO 1979.

8. Described by Boehmer, D. J., 'Fire and life safety: an important feature in one of Toronto's newest and unique complexes', *Canadian Consulting Engineer*, Sept. 1976: 34–6.

Chapter 5 Remembrance of streets past

It is ironic that, at the very moment that the large regional shopping centres of the early 1960s were attempting to reproduce the homogenised conditions of department store floor space, a New York department store should have hit upon the device of a 'street of shops' to break down its sales area into discrete units. Though ignored at first by other New York store operators, the idea of the street as a co-ordinating theme in Geraldine Stutz's experiment at Henri Bendel's was widely taken up in the mid 1970s as a means of creating identity and some sense of orientation in the vast and often confusing floors of trading operations which had grown piecemeal during the course of their history. At Macy's, the largest of them, with each floor covering almost 2 hectares, and a total area, at 200,000 sq. metres, considerably larger than that of most regional centres, Ed Finkelstein, the store's chairman, reconstructed the basement floor along these lines in 1976 as 'The Cellar' with a brick-paved arcade fronted by small booths selling gourmet food, pottery, posters and vitamins. At Bloomingdales, Barbara D'Arcy used a similar feature in the 'B-way', in which cosmetic and fashion accessory departments were ranged down each side of a glittering black and mirrored 'street', paved with black and white marble squares. On another floor of the same store the 'Main Course' again made reference to the 'street of shops' idea, providing a locus for special promotional events, while elaborate mock shop-fronts delineated areas for Charles Jourdain and other designer ranges.

If the concept of a street [5.1], coupled with that of 'chunk merchandising' or the creation of node points of spectacular display features [5.2], provided a useful design framework, it was not simply this organisational benefit which made it the centre-piece of what many operators regarded as the key to the resurgence of the older established downtown stores in cities like New York. Rather it

5.1   Department store 'street'; Macy's, New York.

5.2   'Chunk merchandising': the formation of focal
        displays within the department store floor. Saks,
        Fifth Avenue, New York.

was the ability of the device to act as a focus for what was termed 'visual merchandising', which was, according to the *New York Times*, instrumental in 'transforming the stodgy, family-orientated department store into a virtual amusement park . . . part store, part theater, part center for continuing education' (Kornbluth 1979: 30, 32). Now in adopting the tactic of 'visual merchandising', in which the character of the setting is seen to be vastly more important than, say, the price-competitiveness of the product, the department stores were following a route which had already been pioneered in a number of shopping centres, but shopping centres of a kind quite different from those discussed so far.

In 1893 the sons of Domingo Ghirardelli, an Italian who had established a chocolate manufacturing business in San Francisco, bought a site occupying a city block near the docks. It included the Woolen Mill, one of the oldest factories in the West, and between 1900 and 1916 they built around it a rambling complex of crenellated, white-trimmed brick buildings surmounted by a large illuminated 'Ghirardelli' sign facing across the Bay. In the early 1960s the chocolate manufacturing business was sold and transferred to new works, and the possibility of demolishing the old buildings and redeveloping the 1-hectare site arose. Instead it was acquired by William M. Roth and a group of San Franciscans, and converted to retail use. The central courtyard was excavated to form an underground multi-storey car park, topped by pavilions, canopies and open terraces which linked the old buildings which surrounded them. The architects, Wurster, Bernadi and Emmons, exploited the falls across the site to create a complex of galleries and courts which had to be explored and discovered to be appreciated, and to which the information booth now supplies a guide leaflet for a half-hour walking tour [5.3].

When it opened in 1964 Ghirardelli Square demonstrated for the first time almost all of the characteristic features of what was to be christened the 'specialty centre', and which differed fundamentally from those of the main regional centres. First, in terms of its tenant mix, it concentrated on small, specialist, up-market traders and eating places, and entirely lacked the major magnet stores considered essential to the conventional centres. Of its 93 retail units, 4 sold works of art, 2 children's toys and clothes, 19 were fashion shops, 5 home furnishing, 7 import shops specialising in goods from a single country (Japan, Ireland, Holland, Iran, China, etc.), 6 jewellery shops, 30 specialty shops (kites, pastries, tobacco, glassware, cosmetics, etc.) and no less than 15 restaurants. In addition, 2 units provided a gift wrapping and shipping service for purchases made in the centre, and a cinema and 12 professional office suites were accommodated.

The second characteristic feature lay in its physical form – eccentric, apparently haphazard, inviting exploration, and above all with intriguing historical associations [5.4]. Thirdly, in terms of its location, it was off-pitch in relation to established shopping patterns, and in a declining area, but one which had strong and memorable physical features, and, in particular, proximity to a waterfront. Indeed almost the only trait which it shared with the regional centres was the pertinacity of its

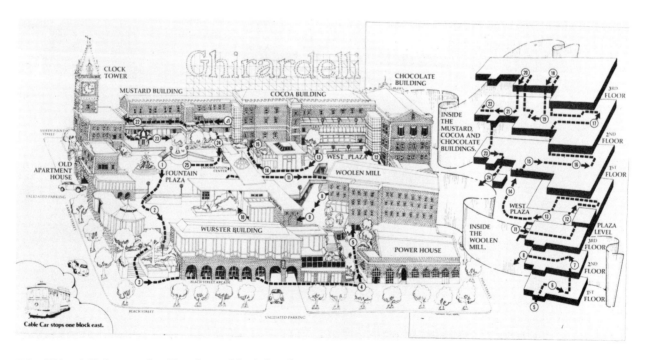

5.3 Ghirardelli Square, San Francisco: visitor's brochure
     describing a half-hour walking tour.

management with regard to promoting the centre, keeping it immaculately clean, and maintaining a calculated tenant mix.

The development and subsequent success of a great number of specialty centres in the United States based on these principles is illustrative of the importance of the mall, or public space, in terms of its psychological rather than its technical performance. For whereas it is possible to describe the evolution of the main centres as a struggle in which the mall gradually asserts its character as a unifying element in the middle of functionally more dominant components, on the back of its mechanical, space-comfort, role, in the specialty centre it is the character of the public space which is itself dominant. There the mall *is* the magnet, which draws shoppers to itself through sheer force of character, despite its off-centre location and as a focus for a collection of traders which, individually, provide a marginal attraction. And the essence of this magnetism is the notion that shopping (at least for non-essential goods and services) can be a pleasurable, social experience, worth indulging for its own sake. That this feature of shopping should be thus isolated, distilled and marketed as a unique ingredient, may be taken as a measure of the compartmentalisation of contemporary life, and

also of the extent to which the shopping street itself could be regarded as a marketable commodity.

The marketing of specialist goods in such a way is probably as old as the luxury trade itself. The Exeter Change was built in 1676 in London to cater for the movement of fashionable society westward towards Covent Garden, and contained elements of pure 'visual merchandising', including the city's only elephant: 'the shops being furnished with such articles as might tempt an idler, or remind a passenger of his wants. At the further end was a man in splendid costume who proved to belong to a menagerie above stairs. A macaw was swinging on a perch above him. . .'.[1] Devices of this kind were present in most of the main centres of the 1960s and 1970s, from the hot-air balloons at Scarborough to the 300-piece full-size mechanical circus (including a robot elephant) at the Northshore Shopping Center in Massachusetts. But the extension of visual merchandising from isolated novelty features to encompass the whole character of a centre, and the proliferation of such centres to meet a mass demand for luxury items coupled with the expression of shopping as a social entertainment, are features peculiar to the development of the specialty centres which followed Ghirardelli Square.

5.4 Ghirardelli Square, San Francisco: view of central space.

Many of the earliest and most famous such centres, such as The Cannery, built a few blocks further east in the San Francisco waterfront area [5.5], Trolley Square in Salt Lake City, and Faneuil Hall in Boston, shared two particular characteristics established by Ghirardelli Square – of attracting a relatively high proportion of out-of-town tourist visitors to a hitherto neglected area, and of linking this to the question of conservation and reuse of old buildings – which proved to be enduring, though not necessarily essential, themes of this form of development. They were the result of brave experiments by isolated entrepreneurs whose vision of a new shopping type was not shared by the institutions which provided funding for conventional centres. It took Benjamin Thompson, architect for the Faneuil Hall Scheme, ten years to get the project to completion, and his developer, the Rouse Company, was obliged to spread the risk over ten banks, despite heavy public sector investment in the project. Such problems were experienced by many of the developers, and are plaintively attested at Pier 39, a later waterfront development in San Francisco's Fisherman's Wharf district, in the plaques set up around the centre relating its history in such terms as

5.5   The Cannery, San Francisco.

THEY SAID: 'IT COULDN'T BE DONE!' Pier 39 is the first privately financed development on San Francisco's Waterfront to be approved and constructed in over 100 years. Major companies such as US Steel, Ford Motor Company, the Rockefellers and Dillingham all tried, and failed, to win approval over the years. Yet Warren Simmons, the local 'little guy' developer, managed to wade Pier 39 through the 16 governmental agency approvals necessary before construction could begin. But, it wasn't easy! Some said he slept with his slide show under his pillow and mumbled 'Pier 39, Pier 39' in his sleep. There wasn't a service club, luncheon group, garden club or improvement association that he didn't spend an hour or two with. He was told over and over, 'It can't be done' 'The big boys couldn't, how do you expect to get permits? – 'Save your energy and go back to your tacos.' You're standing here now. The pessimists were wrong.

The initiative to develop the Faneuil Hall project arose out of the decision of the Boston Redevelopment Authority (BRA) in 1964 to acquire the three parallel blocks of the old market buildings, within an area of some 2.7 hectares, which had once formed the centre of the city's harbour and wholesale food activity, for demolition and redevelopment. Located close to the city core, but in a state of dereliction and decay, the granite buildings had been erected by the city Mayor, Josiah Quincy, in 1825–26 to the designs of Alexander Parris, and subsequently altered and adapted over the years. The BRA then responded to local pressure to retain the existing buildings, and obtained federal funding through the Department of Housing and Urban Development to do so, expending some $10 million to restore their external structure to its original state. After a first abortive attempt to appoint a developer to turn the buildings to commercial use, based upon the ideas of the Boston architect Benjamin Thompson, the Rouse Company of Columbia, Maryland, took on the project, spending a further $30 million to create some 50,000 sq. metres of retail, office and ancillary space [5.6]. Rouse estimated that their costs were about 30 per cent higher than would have been the case for a new building, but that the exercise yielded rents at three times the national average, of which 25 per cent is returned to the city as ground rent on the ninety-nine-year lease.[2]

The commercial success of Faneuil Hall, attracting some 12 million visits per year [5.7; 5.8], each lasting an average of one and a half hours and yielding $6 of sales, and divided equally between visitors from Greater Boston and those from further afield,[3] was undoubtedly due to the particular style of operation which architect, developer and traders brought to the project, and which has been extensively analysed by Jane McC. Thompson (1979):

The Marketplace, with food as the common denominator, is a mothering place, welcome and supportive, a source of sustenance. . . . Refuting the trend toward homogenization, its shops, owners, voices, and accents all communicate 'Boston'. . . . Shopping for daily necessities, potentially a chore, is elevated to a social pleasure and an understanding of people engaged in daily work. Real life becomes theater.

Thompson (1979) cites six inherent qualities which generate its attraction:

1. People and Activity are inherent: . . . initial animation attracts outside people, who attract more people, which allows the conditions of social interaction that are basically satisfying. As important as the presence of people is the arrangement of people for visibility. . . .

2. Real Utility: The Marketplace offers goods and services that substantially relate to daily need. . . .

3. A Real Environment: . . . Great effort has gone into avoiding the pretense and fakery that is so prevalent in American pseudo-period commercial design. . . .

4. Inherent Novelty and Change: . . . street theater and seasonal displays and promotions add to this changing texture, but they are not as important as the pervasive, if subtle, evolutions of day, night, seasons and people.

5. Inherent Esthetic Pleasure and Sense of Quality: . . . there is impact on all the senses from the stimuli of goods and of people. There is also pleasure to be derived from the built elements, both old and new: rhythmic facades, design of streets, sparkeling lights, feathery trees, soft planting, colors against the grey

granite and red brick. . . . In a world of the shoddy, people respond to quality, because it expresses the investment of time, money and attention. It tells them that somebody cares.

6. Genuine Meaning in the Urban context: . . . Despite its private ownership it is not a private enclave . . . it has been designed to reinforce the vitality of the city's downtown by giving it a needed focal point and by answering its many needs at an intimate and personal scale.

It is worth quoting these criteria at length, since they not only describe well the particular atmosphere of Faneuil Hall, with its integrity of detail in which new and old parts cleanly meet, and careful control of tenants' features ('The tenant may not use coy, rustic or unnaturally antiquated names or use imitations of old English or other scripts or affectations of spelling'[4]), but also because, as a general description of subsequent American specialty centres, they are startlingly idealised and unachieved qualities. For of the great majority of such centres, whose development was encouraged by the success of Ghirardelli Square and Faneuil Hall, it must be said that their activity is not inherent but induced; that they offer goods and services superfluous to daily need; that their

5.6 Faneuil Hall, Boston: view of the central of the three parallel blocks forming the Marketplace.

5.7 Faneuil Hall, Boston: interior view of lightweight
structures clipped to outside of original stone
buildings.

5.8 Faneuil Hall, Boston: stalls in the space between
the blocks.

environment enthusiastically embraces 'pretense and fakery'; that their novelty and sense of quality are self-consciously cultivated; and that they have little real meaning in their urban context. The fact is that they were not, as Jane Thompson would have preferred, the expression of some deeply rooted urban culture, but rather a response to surplus suburban wealth, in which $1 in every $3 spent on food would be spent in restaurants. They thus had more in common with the theme park than the indigenous corner shop, although by their association with issues of urban renewal, conservation and architectural historicism they provide a particularly revealing commentary on aspects of mall design which have a wider significance.

Ghirardelli Square with its centralised courtyard form, and Faneuil Hall with its linear parallel arcades, provided two generic patterns of organisation upon which subsequent specialty centres wove more or less elaborate variations – in effect the village square and the village street. These planning forms were interpreted with differing degrees of ingenuity and success, but it was the visual theme adopted in each case which provides the immediate and dominant impression of each place. Thus on the waterfront at Oakland, across the bay from San Francisco, we find Jack London's log cabin transposed from the Far North

5.10 Jack London Village, Oakland, California: view across central court from south.

5.9 Jack London Village, Oakland, California: view across central court from north.

5.11 Jack London Village, Oakland, California: plan.
1 : 3,000.

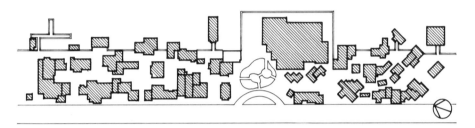

5.12 Ports O'Call Village, Los Angeles: plan. 1 : 3,000.

5.13 Ports O'Call Village, Los Angeles: view.

to establish the theme for a highly planted timber mining camp [*5.9*; *5.10*], of courtyard plan [*5.11*], which forms the specialty centre which bears his name. At San Pedro on the Los Angeles Harbor, Ports O'Call took an attenuated linear form, on a 350-metre-long strip between a road and the waterfront [*5.12*], and adopted a mixture of New England sea-coast and Mississippi steamboat architecture [*5.13*; *5.14*]. Some seventy-eight timber 'houses' defined a meandering network of brick-paved lanes, punctuated at the midpoint by a Hawaiian pool crossed by bridges and next to the Ports O'Call restaurant, the largest building in the group and the nearest to a 'magnet' unit.

The New England fishing village was one favoured visual theme of the specialty centre, and is even to be found in New England itself, as in the looped street of Pickering Wharf at Salem, Massachusetts [*5.15*; *5.16*]. Another is the pantiles, rendered walls and heavy timber members of the Mexican or Spanish-American hacienda which is to be found in specialty centres scattered across the south-western states, as in the linked courtyards of Prune Yard in San Jose [*5.17*], the small cluster of The Plazas at First Western Square in Las Vegas [*5.18*], and the street and circular plaza of Westbury Square in Houston [*5.19*]. An English shambles may be discovered next to the *Queen Mary* (itself a kind of specialty centre with

restaurants and gift boutiques) on Long Beach, Los Angeles, while a fragment of a French provincial town was built in Columbus, Ohio, where The Continent [*5.20*] offers apartments for sale over the shops and an enclosed market building specialising in French food.

In each of these cases a new development has been clad in a traditional style, which, if not always totally foreign to the region, is at least a relatively self-conscious attempt to package the selling place in a way distinctly different from the modernism of the main centres, and with as much exuberance and explorable detail as might be crammed within the available budget. That such overtly historicist props were not essential to the success of the specialty centre theatre was demonstrated by a relatively smaller number of examples, which tended to come after the first wave of refurbishment projects and the second wave of their historicist imitators. Thus Pier 39, forming a street of shingle-clad pavilions running out into the San Francisco Bay [*5.21*], was more subdued in its vernacular display [*5.22*], as was the Willows at Concord across the Oakland Bridge [*5.23*; *5.24*], a centre which serves a more purely local market of new residential areas separated from the established centres of Oakland and San Francisco by the hills of the Diablo Range. Returning to San Francisco's waterfront, the Anchorage Center, cutting diagonally through a city

5.14 Ports O'Call Village, Los Angeles: view.

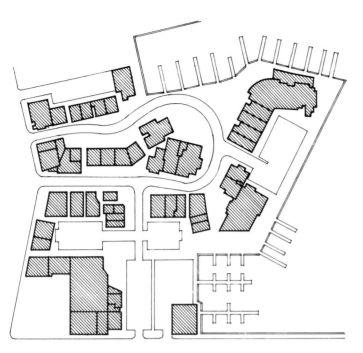

5.15 Pickering Wharf, Salem, Mass.: plan. 1 : 3,000.

5.16 Pickering Wharf, Salem, Mass.: view of entrance
building.

5.17 Prune Yard, San Jose, California: view.

5.18 The Plazas at First Western Square, Las Vegas,
      Nevada : view.

5.19 Westbury Square Shopping Village, Houston,
Texas: view of central plaza.

5.20 The Continent, Columbus, Ohio: view of main
street.

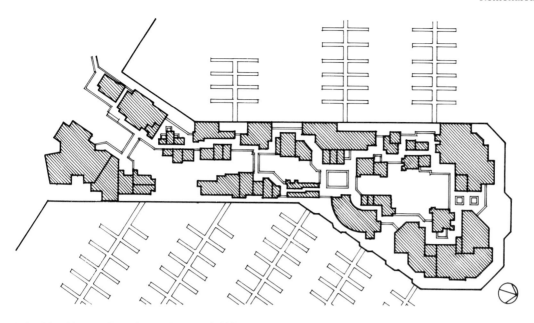

5.21 Pier 39, San Francisco: plan. 1 : 3,000.

5.22 Pier 39, San Francisco: view.

5.23 The Willows, Concord, California: view.

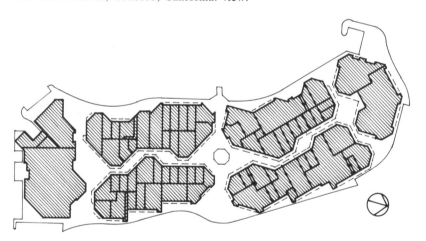

5.24 The Willows, Concord, California: plan. 1 : 3,000.

block and building upon the now firmly established tourist draw of the area, was sufficiently confident to abandon vernacular trappings altogether [5.25]. But it was the Faneuil Hall team once more, the Rouse Company and Benjamin Thompson Associates, which convincingly demonstrated that the principles Jane Thompson described could operate without the benefit of a revered existing building, in an untried location, and without any reference to nostalgic visual props.

The renewal of the Inner Harbor area of Baltimore has been a subject of study since the 1950s, when the Charles Center urban renewal programme began a shift in public investment southward from the central business district towards the waterfront where the city had begun in 1729. During the 1970s a series of large, individual buildings began to establish themselves around the Inner Harbor basin, including I. M. Pei's twenty-eight-storey World Trade Center tower, Cambridge

5.25 The Anchorage, San Francisco: view.

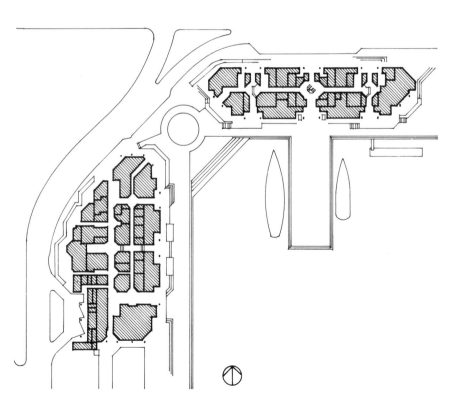

5.26 Harborplace, Baltimore, Maryland: plan of ground
     level. 1 : 3,000.

5.27 Harborplace, Baltimore, Maryland: view of Light Street Pavilion beyond prow of USS *Constellation* moored in basin.

Seven Associates' National Aquarium, the Maryland Science Center, and several office, hotel and conference buildings. In this sense then the location of a shopping centre, Harborplace, in the area was not an isolated gesture. In terms of creating a live public place among the new monoliths, however, the introduction of retail use was important, while in conventional retailing judgement the location seemed at best uncertain. In these circumstances the choice of a specialty centre, on the lines of Faneuil Hall, with its relative independence of existing shopping patterns and its more demonstrative celebration of shopping as a public activity was made.

Despite the historic location, the site lacked the existing buildings suitable for conversion which had featured in the Boston and San Francisco waterfront areas. Instead the architects built two new structures whose form recalled the archetypes of framed dockside warehouses or market halls, but without any apology for their modern construction. Not attempting to define streets or squares, they stand, like the other new buildings nearby, as isolated pavilions, surrounded by the public terraces of the harbourside [5.26]. Their effectiveness lies firstly in setting out a robust and simple vocabulary for the basic building shells, equivalent to the trabeated stone construction of the Faneuil Hall

buildings, but now formed in concrete frame and steel roof expressed clearly both inside and out [5.27; 5.28], and establishing an overall scale to the pavilions appropriate to their exposed setting. This shell was then filled out according to the principles of specialty centre theatre employed at Boston, with glazed wall panels, projecting lean-to roofs and open balconies creating a transparent, show-case exterior, while the interior [5.29] was densely packed with two storeys of booths and stalls lining narrow routes articulated by occasional double-height linking spaces. Set at right angles to each other, at the inner corner of the harbour, the two pavilions were differentiated in their internal arrangement. One, the Light Street Pavilion, with some ninety units, was deeper in plan, and accommodated a preponderance of food traders of various kinds, ranging from restaurants, through some thirty fast-food outlets in the Food Hall, to specialised grocery stalls. The Pratt Street Pavilion, with forty-seven units, concentrated on fashion, gift and similar sales, though it included a further six restaurants which, as in the first pavilion, were around its perimeter, opening on to external terraces.

The simplicity of shell treatment at Harborplace, similar to the straightforward structures adopted by Rouse for many of their main centres such as the

5.28 Harborplace, Baltimore, Maryland: terraces and
restaurants on edge of pavilion facing the harbour.

Mall in Columbia, Hulen Mall and the White
Marsh Center, coupled with the densely packed
and carefully orchestrated liveliness of the fitting
out, formed an effective reminder of the principles
which underlie the creation of social shopping
spaces, both inside and out, and were an
immediate commercial success. Costing $20 million
to construct, the pavilions were estimated to have
earned $42 million turnover in their first year of
operation and to have attracted more visitors, at 18
million, than Disney World.[5] Although entirely
modern in construction, the building shells have the
archetypal character of the nineteenth-century
industrial or commercial buildings which Benjamin
Thompson might have expected to find on the site,
and which have formed the basis of subsequent
projects by his firm, notably St Anthony Main in a
disused mattress factory on the banks of the
Mississippi in Minneapolis [5.30].

Two specialty centres in England provide an
interesting comparison with these American
examples, since both, at Covent Garden in London
and the Piece Hall in Halifax, are housed in
substantial historic buildings comparable in
importance to Faneuil Hall. In contrast to the
American cases, however, both were undertaken by
public authorities rather than private developers,
and in both the consumption of large quantities of

5.29 Harborplace, Baltimore, Maryland: view of interior.

81

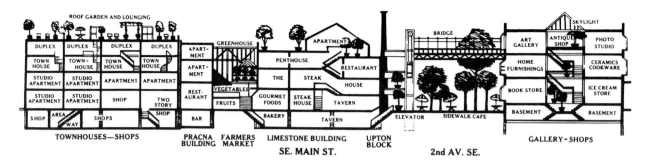

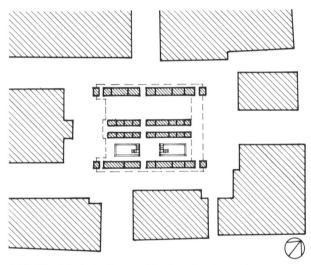

5.30 St Anthony Main, Minneapolis: architect's
explanatory section. (Courtesy Benjamin Thompson
Associates)

5.31 The Market, Covent Garden, London: plan.
1 : 3,000.

food, which plays such an important, and even
reverential, part in the American operations, is
peripheral.

The original Central Market Building at Covent
Garden, designed by Charles Fowler and opened in
1830, comprised three parallel ranges of buildings
linked at their east end by a colonnade [5.31].
Further colonnades ran down the outer side of each
flank of the side ranges, while the middle one
contained a central arcade, 5 metres wide and
rising to clerestory lights above the upper floor of
its two-storey section [5.32]. Fifty years later the
two courtyards lying between the wings were
spanned by glazed, cast-iron framed roofs to
provide a fully covered market building. With the
removal of the fruit and vegetable market to
Battersea in 1974, the Greater London Council
decided to renovate the buildings as small shops,
and after a debate similar to that which took place
in Boston, as to precisely which point in their
history the buildings should be restored, the work
was completed in 1980. The treatment was less
freely adaptive, more scholarly and correct, than at
Faneuil Hall [5.33], with the opening up of sections

of the basement structure to form lower courtyards
in the south hall as the only major departures from
the 1880 formation [5.34]. Shop-fronts were carried
out as part of the landlord's work, based on
original designs salvaged at the beginning of the
restoration.

The success of the Covent Garden Market, and
its access to a huge tourist catchment have, as in so
many American cases, driven its traders up-market,
replacing the 'indigenous' chemists, bookbinders
and theatre support industries of the area with a
preponderance of luxury and impulse outlets. In
this it contrasts with the Piece Hall in Halifax
which retains the more modest and casual
atmosphere of a local market. The building is not a
hall as such, but a splendid quadrangle [5.35], with
continuous open galleries on its inner sides giving
access to rows of small units which were
constructed in 1779 for the display and sale of local
manufacturers' 'pieces' or lengths of woollen and
worsted cloth. The central courtyard falls across the
site, giving three levels of galleries in the lower half
of the quadrangle, and two in the upper, all within
a constant roof line. The treatment of the arcades
becomes progressively lighter as they rise up the
building, with an arched gallery at the base,
rusticated piers in the centre and slender Doric
columns at the top, and the whole arrangement
seems designed for the display of people, at varying
levels within and across the central court, as a
foreground to merchandise, and hence a peculiarly
appropriate setting for a specialty centre. Restored
and reopened for this purpose in 1976, at a cost of
£354,000, it accommodates forty-three mainly craft,
antiques and bric-à-brac units around the perimeter
building, with removable stalls for a weekend open-
air market in the central courtyard [5.36].

As in the USA, these first experiments in
specialty centres within renovated existing buildings
have been followed by plans for purpose-built
centres in the UK, the first being on the site of the
Waverley Markets in the centre of Edinburgh.
Situated at one end of the open, gardens side of
Princes Street, its form is dominated by the Act of

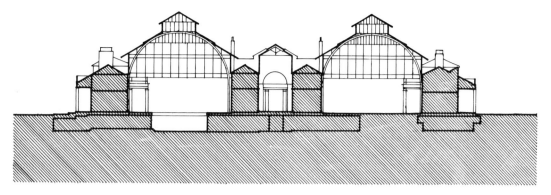

5.32 The Market, Covent Garden, London: section.
   1 : 600.

5.33 The Market, Covent Garden, London: view from
   west.

Parliament which requires any such construction to rise no more than 1 metre above pavement level. It is thus a subterranean centre, its floors dropping down within the valley section below an upper open terrace at the Princes Street level, and punctuated by voids which bring light down from glazed elements on this terrace [5.37; 5.38].

The comparatively small number of purpose-built specialty centres in Europe disguises the fact that a similar function is performed in existing quarters and in circumstances which have raised the same questions of conservation, encouragement of indigenous traders, and urban renewal, which have marked the American examples. Whole areas of

many European cities, such as York, Chester or the New Town of Edinburgh, have become, in effect, specialty centres, dependent on out-of-town visitors, trading in non-essential goods, and subject to painstaking development control to maintain or restore the historic theatre they supply. In introducing the consultants' planning report for the city of Chester, Sir George Grenfell-Baines' observation that 'Chester's face is her fortune'[6] is a concise prescription for the application of visual merchandising to a whole town.

This notion has gradually been extended to include not only outstanding historic sites, but indeed any centre in which the shopping area can

5.34 The Market, Covent Garden, London: view of
sunken courtyards formed in south hall.

5.35 Piece Hall, Halifax, England: view from upper
gallery of central courtyard.

5.36 Piece Hall, Halifax, England: Sunday market in
central courtyard.

be regarded as a co-ordinated, managed environment with some inherent and locally appreciated visual character. An important factor in encouraging this tendency has been the widespread adoption of pedestrianisation projects, which began tentatively and with considerable reservations among affected shopkeepers, and have since come to be regarded as an essential feature by which the city centre can compete with newer suburban centres, in much the same way that the formation of proper pavements restored the competitiveness of established shops in the centre of Paris in the nineteenth century in relation to recently constructed pedestrian arcades.[7] Seen at first as a purely technical device for removing conflict between wheeled and pedestrian movements in congested routes such as London Street in Norwich, first closed to traffic in 1965, pedestrianisation later came to be recognised as a means by which a street could be managed, visually

and in trading terms, as a co-ordinated enterprise – in effect a mall. The continuity of paving from shop-front to shop-front, the installation of special lighting, signage and street furniture, and the achievement of a greater intimacy of scale by the introduction of planting, booths and other features within the street space, all encouraged the view of the street as a place of destination, rather than simply a necessary corridor.

This intention is exemplified by the case of Munich, in which a relative decline in the market share of the central shopping area, due to traffic congestion and the post-war growth of suburban shopping centres and hypermarkets, led to the sponsoring of a competition for the design of a pedestrian system for the city centre, spurred by the impending 1972 Olympic Games in the city. The first phase comprised the pedestrianisation of the main east–west street through the original medieval core, Neuhauserstrasse and Kaufingerstrasse, running some 700 metres between the old town gates of Karlstor to the west and Rathaus to the east. This was subsequently extended to cross-streets, to create a network articulated by focal points responding to the pattern of existing streets and buildings [5.39].

Impressed by both the commercial and visual success of examples such as Munich, a great number of towns and cities have undertaken pedestrianisation projects, ranging in extent from the simple exclusion of cars, to the complete enclosure of existing streets. The success of such schemes has varied according to a number of local factors, but has generally depended upon the degree of acknowledgement by the implementing authority that they were engaged in a process very similar to that of any mall developer. That is, that the street, formerly an expedient assembly of individual owners, was now to be treated as a single managed enterprise, to be designed, funded, managed and promoted like any other. What began as an exercise in traffic control thus turned out to

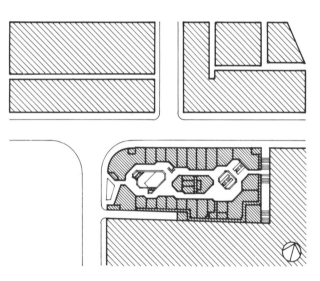

5.37 Waverley Market, Edinburgh: plan. 1 : 3,000.

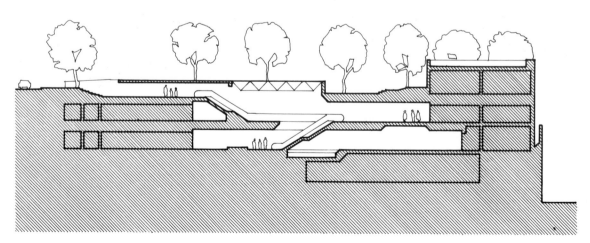

5.38 Waverley Market, Edinburgh: section across the development, north–south, with Princes Street on the left. 1 : 600.

involve the extension of questions of the design and management of public space from the restricted territory of the shopping mall out into the city as a whole. Since these projects involved little in the way of trading or user space, and were almost entirely concerned with the treatment of the public areas between existing frontages, they provide a fascinating catalogue of attempts by designers to symbolise, with whatever landscaping or quasi-sculptural elements might be devised, all of the qualities of diversity, continuity, imageability, monumentality or intimacy which might be associated with a successful public place. The repertoire of devices which could be employed to this end was exemplified by Rossetti Associates project for Washington Boulevard in Detroit, in which the once-fashionable street was refurbished by restricting vehicles to one side of the former eight-lane width, and creating a five-block-long pedestrian area down the other [5.40]. Using steel

pergolas, steps which turned into miniature amphitheatres, fountains, soft landscaping and the paraphernalia of street furniture, the designers created a kind of abstract set for the street theatre which was intended to occur [5.41].

Now in all these examples, from the American specialty centres to the numerous conservation and pedestrianisation projects in existing city streets, the relevance to this study of the mall and street designs lies not so much in their forms, which are generally based upon simple historical types, as in the questions they raise about the ways in which the shopping mall can and should relate to its surrounding city context. To a large extent the answers they provide are partial and full of contradictions, providing ammunition for diametrically opposed views as to their success. If the industrialised suburban shopping mall in all its variations may be seen as the development of the nineteenth-century arcade, which began as a

5.39 Neuhauser Strasse, Munich: view of pedestrianised
    street, towards Karlstor, the former city gate.

5.40 Washington Boulevard, Detroit: view of overall
   project. (Courtesy Gino Rossetti Associates)

5.41 Washington Boulevard, Detroit: space-defining
structures in the pedestrianised zone. (Courtesy
Gino Rossetti Associates)

subservient link between established frontages, to the point where it has absorbed and supplanted the essential dynamic of urban shopping, these projects provide an ambiguous critique of how such a situation might be restored.

In their emphasis upon the liveliness of the building façade, upon an intimacy of building scale, and above all upon the renovation, reconstruction or reproduction of historic settings, they challenge the external blankness and internal blandness of the industrialised mall. Yet such preferences are themselves acts of design, as calculated as any other. In the process of renewal old buildings are inevitably changed and set in a more precious, more contrived light. At its best, this process, as at Faneuil Hall, may be seen as a frankly expressed stage in the continuing life of a valued structure, but at its worst it degenerates into what one critic has called 'the new kitsch of advanced capitalism, self-conscious for all of its charm, and boring for all of its originality',[8] or another, 'part of that grand and endlessly running British cultural project to make the institutions of the present day seem like those of pre-industrial, agrarian, village society',[9] a spurious titillation matching the exotic triviality of the goods they sell.

Again, in their location in neglected and declining city areas they are seen as a powerful agent of urban renewal in contrast to the destructive influence of the green-field centre. This optimistic view has been strongly argued by James Rouse for whom the success of projects like Faneuil Hall and the Baltimore Harborplace represents 'the edge of a big transformation of the central city. Reports of the death of the American city were premature. The American city isn't dying. It's being reborn . . . the task of making the American city a fit place to grow our people is the No. 1 priority of our civilization' in the achievement of which, 'profit is the thing that hauls dreams into focus'.[10] Again however, the process of resuscitation also involves change, which as in the arguments over conservation, is seen by critics as either destroying or else superficially camouflaging the thing to be saved. At Covent Garden, the Market building stands at the heart of an area which was to be comprehensively redeveloped until opposition resulted in the abandonment of the scheme and its replacement by a policy of piecemeal renewal and rehabilitation. Activists who had argued that the pressures of redevelopment would destroy the local community, now suggest that they were merely diverted into an alternative form, that of 'gentrification' (in America, cruelly, 'Faneuilisation') with the same effect of displacing the local social and economic structure. For all their difficulties in getting the Faneuil Hall project moving, and their care in encouraging local, single-outlet traders to dominate the tenant mix, Benjamin Thompson Associates have subsequently expressed doubts about the ability of specialty centres to retain this priority.[11] Ironically this is a

result of their success, by which they have come to be seen by retail developers as another reproducable centre type, which can be let to chain operators identical to those found in other developments up and down the country. Are such centres, unlikely colonists of derelict waterfront or inner-city areas, then to be regarded as the spearhead of some wider regeneration, or are they simply outposts of the suburban economy, located where they are for reasons of ambience and cheap site costs, and displacing the problems of the area to some other place?

Finally, in terms of urban design, such projects have been held to show the ways in which the retail element can act as a catalyst for the reconstruction of a more humane and integrated urban environment, in contrast to the 'no-place' of the free-standing, stereotyped mall, which has been instrumental in the dispersal and standardisation of the city's functions. And again this claim has been subject to heated debate. The pedestrianisation of Kaufingerstrasse led to a new sense of cohesion in the central core of Munich and to its physical resurgence. But although this is the 'real' city in terms of its historical form and geographical location, it is cut off from the surrounding city by the inner ring road and by those very characteristics of pedestrianisation and historical restoration which have saved it. In this sense it seems 'unreal' in the context of the present city, an independent theme centre which just happens to have been located in the middle of town. Similarly the linear pattern of streets at Faneuil Hall now leads nowhere, since the waterfront which once formed their termination and rationale is now separated from them by the Fitzgerald Expressway, and in the context of downtown Boston it is the markets, rather than the new towers, which seem strangely rootless.

Undoubtedly many of these criticisms are unfair or premature. How could the social fabric of Covent Garden be preserved when its economic base, the wholesale market, had been removed? And how can a single shopping centre be expected to regenerate a whole local economy or restore an urban fabric torn by motorways and crude redevelopment projects? Instead, it has been suggested,[12] they should be regarded, not as the harbingers of a new social and planning order, but as the equivalent of the parks which nineteenth-century planners introduced into the city as a carefully contrived memory of the nature which the city had displaced. Now, however, it is not nature, but an image of the city itself, in an earlier and more urbane form, which is to be cultivated and preserved.

It is perhaps the highly visible and theatrical element of these projects, epitomised in their historicism, which has so attracted disparagement, encapsulated in their almost inevitable comparison to Disneyland. There is considerable justice in this comparison. Not only is the Rouse Company said to have benefited from studying Disney's maintenance and management methods (scraping up discarded chewing gum on sticks with attached razor blades), but Main Street, the first theme area of the California Disneyland, is, as Richard Francaviglia (1974) has pointed out, a highly controlled piece of urban design. It has a beginning, at the square through which visitors first enter Disneyland, a middle, through the two blocks of the street itself which Disney based upon Marceline, Missouri, and an end, at the plaza where routes lead on to the 'four lands'. Like most purpose-designed shopping centres, whether specialty or main centres, but unlike many pedestrianised high streets, it conforms very well to the criteria Kevin Lynch defined as comprising the imageability of a town, with its clear definition of the elements of edge, path, district, node and landmark (Lynch 1960). But Main Street is also a fantasy, and it is its dream-like quality of make-believe, again shared not only by specialty centres but by many main centre malls as well, which critics find so unpalatable. It seems hard to blame Disneyland or the shopping mall for this. If the picture they present seems to cloy it may be because they are only too embarrassingly accurate mirrors. And if they persistently return to nostalgic images of the town as a legible, charming, safe, clean and sociable public place, it may be because the real town outside is so often the opposite of these things. The dream exists because so also does the nightmare [5.42; 5.43].

Whether the shopping mall can offer more than a romantic critique of the city, and go on to provide effective models of the way public space might be organised on a wider scale, is another question. To investigate this, it will be necessary to examine the mall, not as an isolated form type, but as a pattern of organisation, and to consider how its inherent structure relates to that of the city as a whole.

Notes

1. Robert Southey in 'Letters from England' 1807, quoted from Alison Adburgham, 1964:18.

2. Quoted in 'A boom in recycled buildings', *Business Week*, 31 Oct. 1977:101.

3. Quoted in Robert Campbell, 'Evaluation: Boston's "upper of urbanity"', *AIA Journal*, June 1981: 24–31.

4. Extract from *Retail Tenant Design Criteria*, p. 54, for the North Market, quoted by Robert Campbell, op. cit.

5. From an interview with James Rouse in *Time*, 24 Aug. 1981:42.

6. *Chester–A Plan for the Central Area*, 1964.

7. See Geist 1983:64.

8. Andrew Kopkind, in *The Real Paper*, 19 Feb. 1977, quoted in Suzanne Stephens, 1978:49–53.

9. Richard Hill, 'Architecture: the past fights back', *Marxism Today*, Nov. 1980:24.

10. *Time*, 24 Aug. 1981:46.

11. In an interview with the author, Sept. 1981.

12. See Robert Campbell, op. cit.

5.42 Disneyland, Los Angeles: view along Main Street.

5.43 The Bronx, New York.

Part 2 The mall in the city

Chapter 6 The urban transplant

It has become customary to talk of the crisis of planning in the city in medical terms. Frank Lloyd Wright, Ebenezer Howard and Le Corbusier all spoke of the 'cancer' afflicting contemporary cities, of their 'tumours', 'blocked circulation', 'respiratory failure' and of their 'terminal' condition. The analogy is perhaps helpful in considering the recent development of the shopping mall. It is as if a vital organ had been removed from the ailing patient and then nurtured in isolated, clinical conditions, under which it has been modified and improved according to its own, internal, programme. The problem now arises as to how this new part is to be reintegrated into the parent body without incurring disruption and rejection. The fact that in the UK, for example, the operation was carried out without removing the organ from the body, does not avoid the problem of massive trauma to the fabric surrounding the modified part and its extensive circulation. And if the life support systems seem rather too much in evidence, if the staff maintain an atmosphere of forced cheerfulness, insisting on a sterile environment, rigidly excluding other uses, dictating strict visiting hours, and obsessively maintaining cleanliness and discipline with armies of ward orderlies (the Macy's department stores have a bigger police force than the town of White Plains, with a population of 50,000) for fear of contamination from the open city outside, we may put this down to the severity of the operation.

Having made these allowances however, the side-effects are still disquieting. The gains in comfort and safety made within the mall appear to have been achieved at the expense of the surrounding areas of the city. Strange reversals of frontage have occurred, by which streets formerly lined with shops and activity are now degraded to 'traffic sewers', fronted by car parks, service loading areas and the blank rear walls of shop storage areas from which no amount of architectural modelling can disguise the loss of active meaning. The visible

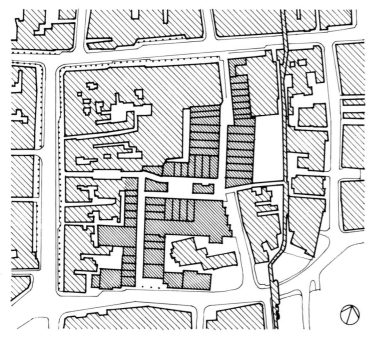

6.1   Grosvenor Centre, Chester: plan at mall level.
      1 : 3,000.

activity of the city has been transferred indoors to a place which, for all its physical proximity to the surrounding streets, is felt to be a separate and isolated precinct, ambiguous in its status as a public place with its own police force and opening hours. Though seeming to offer a generous, all-weather public forum, it is discovered that its activities are carefully screened and restricted to certain acceptable commercial or cultural forms.[1]

In many of the early examples of new 'hearts', as they were often called, built in existing cities in post-war Britain in the form of independent precincts, rather than simply reconstructed bomb-damaged high streets, these disturbing symptoms were not obtrusive. The Grosvenor Centre in Chester, for example, was constructed in the south-east quarter of the city's Roman plan, in land lying behind the two main frontages to Eastgate and Bridge Street. Connecting unobtrusively into these two streets [6.1], in the latter case through an existing Victorian arcade, and using the levels created by their unique two-storey rows, the new development was able to insert some 15,000 sq. metres of retail space, together with basement service access and a 600-space multi-storey car park, almost invisibly into the city fabric, except on the south side of the block, where it emerged from among the existing buildings.

The principle of using relatively cheap, underused back-land, lying behind existing high-value frontages, was not new. It was, after all, one of the means by which Napoleon III and his Prefect, Georges Haussmann, were able to implement their project to construct a great network of new boulevards through the congestion

of nineteenth-century Paris.[2] After years of attempts by earlier officials to carry out road improvement schemes by piecemeal acquisitions and the enforcement of new building lines as individual properties came up for renewal, Haussmann hit upon the more radical strategy of running the boulevards wherever possible through the 'soft' areas which lay behind the crust of established and difficult frontages. In minimising the disturbance to these properties he not only reduced his land costs, but also cleared the slum areas which lay behind, and by the acquisition of additional land on each side of the new roads was able to benefit from the betterment created by them.

This precedent offered a classic pattern for developing new shopping centres within existing towns, and with the particular benefit that the new mall could tap into the existing pedestrian flows with the minimum of acquisition on the high street itself. It was a feature of the early Arndale Centres, which introduced the American industrialised mall to the provincial towns of England. The first of these, the Crossgates Shopping Centre in Leeds, opened in 1967, was, in effect, a Yorkdale 'L' mall plan built within a suburban centre block with two existing retail frontages [6.2], in which the pedestrian flow across the mall entrances on to these frontages acted in the place of terminal magnets. In the Arndale Centre at Luton a linear mall was set out parallel to the main street, with connecting side malls to it and with existing major stores provided with additional rear space which enabled them to open frontages to both street and mall. A similar arrangement was adopted for the Whitgift Centre at Croydon opened in 1969, and, as already described, with the added refinement that a fall across the site between flanking streets allowed it to develop two mall levels, each connected out to the existing circulation.

The principle was particularly acceptable for historic towns, such as Chester, in which the new development could be seen as reinforcing, rather than competing with, the existing fabric. In their scheme for the Chequer Street Development in St Albans, for example, the John S. Bonnington Partnership laid down a network of small lanes within the block [6.3], lined overhead with flats, and leading to a new square in the centre of the former back-land, beyond which the major department store and multi-storey car park elements were accommodated [6.4]. The existing main-street frontages thus became a permeable crust, through archways and small openings in which pedestrians could filter into the new development, the largest and most inflexible elements of which were held furthest away from the small-scale existing streetscape.

The degree to which the highly irregular land and building formations of English towns, and the fluctuating patterns of negotiation and counter-negotiation, made demands upon the ingenuity of architects and developers is heavily marked upon most of these projects. The simple imposition of an industrialised mall plan upon a relatively flat and open site, as at the Crossgates Centre, was rarely possible. Instead, the organisational principles of the new development, so clearly visible in the American out-of-town models and based upon movement patterns between points of entry and magnet stores, had to be accommodated to the complex irregularities of existing sites and modified to meet the sensibilities of existing traders, landowners and interested groups. As Keith Scott (1980), one of the most experienced British architects in this field, has put it,

6.2 Arndale Crossgates Centre, Leeds: aerial view.

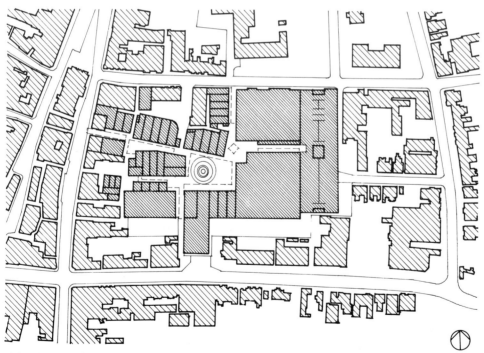

6.3 Chequer Street, St Albans, England: plan of competition proposal by John S. Bonnington Partnership. 1 : 3,000.

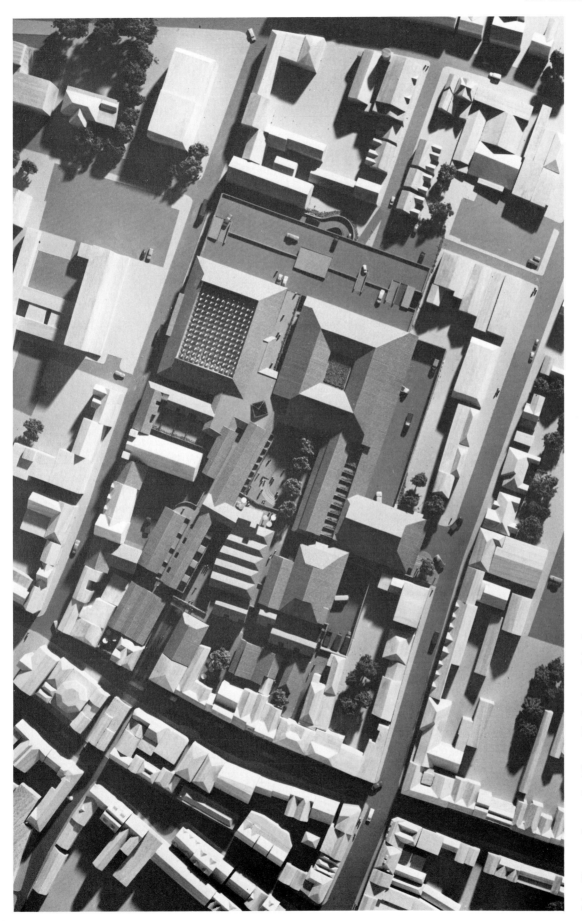

6.4   Chequer Street, St Albans, England: model of competition proposal by John S. Bonnington Partnership. 1 : 3,000. (Courtesy John S. Bonnington Partnership)

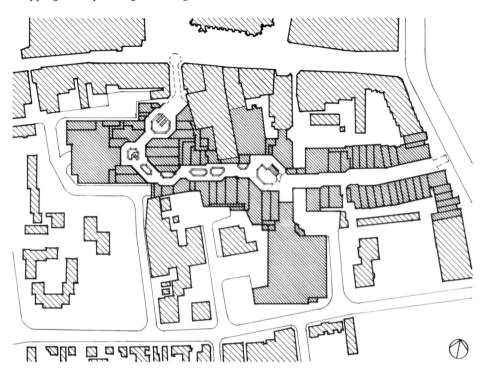

6.5   The Ridings, Wakefield, England: plan taken at varying levels along the mall. 1 : 3,000.

6.6   The Ridings, Wakefield, England: view of interior.

Without question, central area schemes are the toughest nuts to crack. To me it is a continuing miracle that any get built at all. . . . Firstly, there is never a fixed site. . . . You can put money on the probability of its being changed – often, and sometimes radically. . . . Then there is never a fixed brief for the designer to assimilate. The brief evolves from the subtle commercial pressures that shift constantly with time and fashion.

The project by Chapman Taylor Partners for the Ridings in Wakefield well illustrates the impact of these conditions upon the simple principle of back-land development. Following a basic 'L' plan arrangement to connect two points on the existing main shopping streets [6.5], the mall was obliged to undertake a complex series of manoeuvres in order to avoid existing obstructions, and at the same time yield the continuous frontages, balanced tenant mix and clear circulation structure which the development required. With a two-storey level difference between the north entry, at the junction of Westgate and Kirkgate opposite the cathedral, and the east entry, from an existing parade of shops which had been built off lower Kirkgate, the mall rose through three floors, articulated by two main vertical top-lit spaces in which escalators connected the pedestrian levels [6.6]. It similarly undertook a series of directional shifts on plan to stitch a complex assembly of rental spaces around the backs of existing buildings, and one which was capable of being serviced and fed by integral multi-storey car parks.

In one of the largest exercises of this kind, the Queensgate Centre in the middle of the cathedral

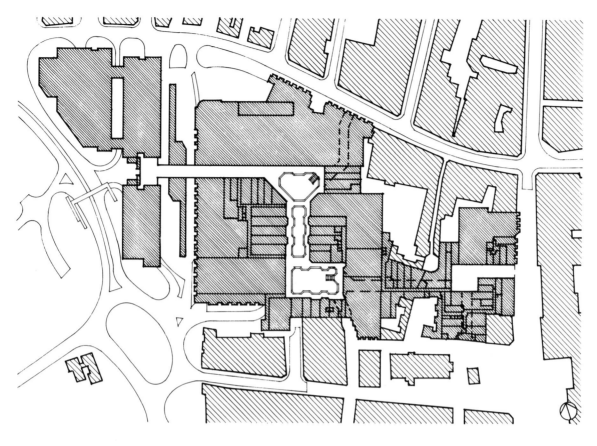

6.7 Queensgate Centre, Peterborough, England: plan at
upper mall level. 1 : 3,000.

city of Peterborough was again contained by
main-street frontages, the greater part of which
were retained. A staggered mall route was set out
through the centre of the block defined by this
perimeter [6.7], extending over a distance of some
400 metres from a multi-storey car park and bus
station on the western edge of the site, against the
inner ring road, to the pedestrianised spaces of
Long Causeway and Cathedral Square on the east.
The mall was given two main levels, generated by
upper-level access from the west and ground level
from the existing frontages on the other three
sides, and these were locked together in the central
zone, stretching between two squares [6.8], in one
of the most convincing UK examples of an
American department store mall space.

Such projects can be viewed as beneficial
intensifications of an existing pattern, in which new
frontage is created by subdividing the former block
arrangement, and developing previously underused
land. They thus appear to complement the existing
city form rather than to contradict it. Thus, on a
smaller scale, the Cofferidge Close development at
Stony Stratford can be seen in this way as a natural
intensification of the historic form of the town,
which was based upon a main street of primary

commercial frontage along the old coaching route,
and a secondary parallel rear service street with
connecting lanes on which supporting service trades
were located. The new development amplified one
of these lanes in the form of a colonnade [6.9;
6.10], leading to less intensive commercial use and
a car park courtyard at the rear, and served from
the secondary rear street. However, such a
symbiosis depends upon certain conditions being
met. It depends firstly upon the relative scale of the
combined network and hence its ability to maintain
active frontage throughout its length; secondly upon
the capacity of the surrounding streets to absorb
the traffic generation of the new areas; and thirdly
upon the ability of the existing fabric to contain the
new building and act as surrogate secondary
frontage to it. That is to say that it requires the
existing town to mask certain features of the new
element which, in its out-of-town condition, can be
treated as marginal side-effects, but which become
altogether more problematic when transplanted into
the city. This becomes most apparent, not on the
strongly established high-street frontages where a
sensitive interjection by the new mall can be
achieved, but in the rear areas where the greatest
traffic movements and most obtrusive mass of car

6.8   Queensgate Centre, Peterborough, England: view of
       interior. (Courtesy Peterborough Development
       Corporation)

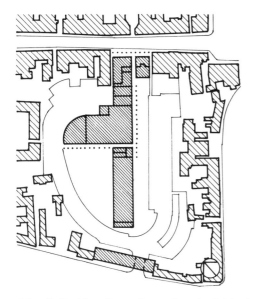

6.9 Cofferidge Close, Stony Stratford, England: plan of development extending back from the High Street, top, to vehicular access from parallel rear street, bottom. 1 : 3,000.

6.10 Cofferidge Close, Stony Stratford, England: arcade leading south from the High Street.

parks and blank shop walls are suddenly exposed against a less cohesive fabric of smaller buildings and streets. It is at these points that the role of the existing buildings as a mask for the new structure becomes most apparent, and doubts occur as to whether the latter does indeed represent simply a more elaborate form of the older pattern, or perhaps instead an altogether different type of animal.

The question became insistent when the scale of the new elements grew to the point where they could no longer be screened by existing buildings, and in such major central area developments as the Arndale Centre in Manchester and the Eldon Square project in Newcastle upon Tyne, the essential differences between old and new patterns of organisation became unavoidably apparent. Of similar size, at around 100,000 sq. metres of retail space, and with sites covering several former city blocks divided in each case by a main thoroughfare, these centres clearly demonstrated two characteristics in particular of the new urban mall – the inversion of frontage and the autonomy of the mall itself – which distinguished it from the older fabric.

If one looks at the building patterns of the two centres before and after redevelopment, the nature of the inversion which has occurred becomes clear. Before redevelopment [6.11; 6.12], the land is subdivided by streets which define blocks, within each of which frontage, and value, are concentrated on the perimeter. With redevelopment [6.13; 6.14], the site perimeter, of whatever shape, is demarcated, and a pedestrian route taken through the centre of the resulting form. The blocks of space thus defined are subdivided into units, with frontage and value concentrated on the central routes. Viewed from the surrounding streets, an alarming reversal of the rules governing the form of the city appears to have occurred. Whereas development once competed for the light, air and access provided by the street, it now has no use for these things [6.15], and instead presents the blank, scaleless panels of its rear walls, whose only function is to insulate the interior as soundly as possible. In the Newcastle development a major public space, Eldon Square, was retained, wrapped on three sides by the new building. Yet despite its sympathetic architectural treatment, with terraces and colonnades to match the scale of the space, its significance as a public place has gone, since the surrounding buildings have all turned to face the other way. The grand architectural statement and almost central location only serve to underline the loss of meaning.

As regards the autonomy of the mall, a similar sectional organisation in both schemes again demonstrates in a vivid way the change which has occurred. In such projects within an existing city, the mall circulation is, as has been noted, necessarily locked into the existing pedestrian flows,

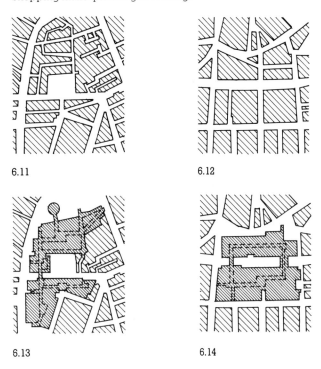

6.11

6.12

6.13

6.14

6.11 Newcastle upon Tyne: site of Eldon Square Centre before redevelopment.
6.12 Manchester: site of Arndale Centre before redevelopment.
6.13 Newcastle upon Tyne: site of Eldon Square Centre after redevelopment.
6.14 Manchester: site of Arndale Centre after redevelopment.

which act in a parallel capacity to the huge surface car parks of the out-of-town centres, as feeders for the system. But the mall is dependent upon those flows only at intermittent points of entry from adjoining high streets, bus stations and car parks, between which it is free to adopt its own preferred alignments which tend, for reasons of flexibility in the subdivision of the surrounding tenant spaces, to be strictly horizontal. Where there is a fall across the site, this tendency invites the application of a mall datum which corresponds to street level on the higher ground, and allows the introduction of service access and accommodation below it on the lower ground. In the vertical plane as well as the horizontal therefore, the existing features of the site become a boundary constraint defining a development volume, through the middle of which the mall is free to adopt its own configuration, making contact with the perimeter at occasional, pre-selected points.

In both the Newcastle and Manchester projects this autonomy of the mall is revealed outside the building at points where existing streets cross the sites, and are traversed at high level by malls which have detached themselves from grade [6.16]. The axis of primary activity is then shown to be removed from its customary location on section as well as plan, and the existing street a hazard which it is obliged to bridge.

In these projects the constraints of complex and irregular sites, and the tradition in most post-war British urban developments of accommodating the

6.15 Arndale Centre, Manchester: external street frontages on Cannon Street dominated by traffic.

6.16 Arndale Centre, Manchester: view of north-west
corner, with blank external walls of main shopping
level crossing Cannon Street on the right, and
pedestrian footbridge at mall level crossing
Corporation Street on the left.

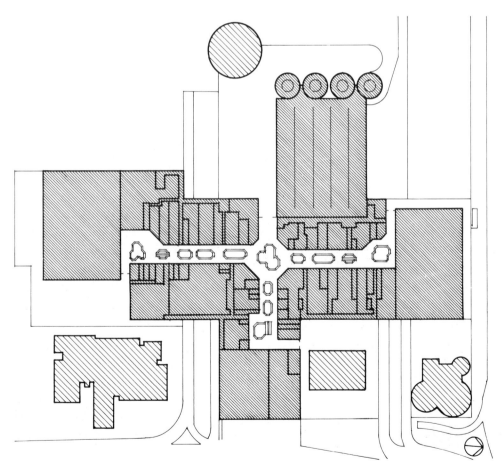

6.17 La Part-Dieu, Lyons: plan at mall level 2. 1 : 3,000.

new in more or less ingenious configurations to the old, so that they become locked together in a Laocoön-like union, hides the generic identity of the urban mall with its out-of-town counterpart. Elsewhere, however, central area projects have made that relationship explicit in couplings of a less contingent kind. In Lyons, the Part-Dieu redevelopment of some thirty-two blocks of the irregular gridiron of the city on the left bank of the Rhône, on the site of a former barracks, included a regional shopping centre whose cruciform mall plan precisely reflected the transposition of a form developed in the out-of-town condition into a central area context [6.17]. Providing some 110,000 sq. metres of retail space on three main mall levels, the CCR (Centre Commercial Régional) preserved the classic plan form and internal character of a 'department store' mall, but now supported by the more intensive forms of multi-storey parking for its 4,500 cars and underground servicing for its shops, made necessary by the restrictions of the urban site. In common with other office, hotel and conference buildings on the site, the CCR was treated as a free-standing object, fulfilling its description as 'un super-paquebot urbain'[3] which happened to have berthed in a downtown harbour. To the characteristics of frontage inversion and mall autonomy, La Part-Dieu and other similar projects thus brought a third feature, that of figure-ground reversal, in which the pattern of solids and voids in the city plan abruptly changes at the boundary of the development area, and with it that long-debated transformation in the character of public space in the city in which its former intimate connection to building frontage is altogether removed.

The implications of these three basic characteristics of the *super-paquebot urbain* could hardly be avoided, even where its perimeter shell was made to conform to the building lines of established city blocks, as occurred in a number of North American centres built within the relatively narrow blocks of a gridiron street plan. The development of a linear two-level mall down the centre of a series of such blocks at Main Place, Buffalo, for example [6.18], effectively relegated the flanking street to the status of a garbage trucking way. Less brutal in its treatment, though similar in form, the Plaza Pasadena in Los Angeles, California, presents the aspect of an Islamic compound to the surrounding town, protecting its interior gardens and painted halls [6.19; 6.20],

6.18 Main Place, Buffalo, New York: view of exterior.

6.19 Plaza Pasadena, Los Angeles: view of mall court.

6.20 Plaza Pasadena, Los Angeles: interior of vaulted entry.

6.21 Plaza Pasadena, Los Angeles: view of exterior.

6.22 Plaza Pasadena, Los Angeles: view of vaulted entry facing City Hall across Colorado Boulevard.

6.23 The Galleria, White Plains, New York: view of central atrium.

within a muscular masonry shell [6.21], punctuated by a monumental arched gateway acknowledging the city hall across the road [6.22].

The contrast between peremptory exterior, inviting contact only at limited points of entry, and seductive interior, continuously adjusting itself to achieve a maximum exposure, is again striking at The Galleria, in White Plains, New York. Extending, like Buffalo Main Place, between the rigid site lines of flanking streets, it passes over one cross-street in order to form a route between department stores at each end. At its centre is located its most lavish space, an atrium rising through four levels, and surrounded and crossed by open eating areas, water, and plants [6.23]. The contrast between the elaboration of this space and the abruptness of the external perimeter [6.24], could hardly be greater, with the former expanding within the latter's screen like a hidden vortex which reaches down through the upper trading floors to touch street level and suck activity into the interior.

In such projects the relational difficulties of old and new are not caused by a marked difference of scale between the two, but by the inherently different principles of organisation which they adopt. Thus at Santa Monica Place the building occupies a pair of city blocks combined to form a readily digestable unit in the existing pattern. But in its disposition of uses within the site it exactly reverses the customary arrangement. Whereas, in the adjoining blocks, frontage occurs around the

6.24 The Galleria, White Plains, New York: view of
exterior on Main Street.

perimeter, with a concentration of activity and
value at the corners where access to passing traffic
is greatest [6.25], frontage is now located down the
internal axes [6.26]. The highest levels of activity
and accessibility now accrue to the centre, while
the corners become the sites for the lowest-value
uses – multi-storey car parks and the rear areas of
department stores. The skew alignment of the
internal circulation at Santa Monica Place further
reinforces its independence of the external
constraints and when it reaches the perimeter it
crashes through, demolishing the street façade
[6.27]. Now the organisational principles of Santa
Monica Place are essentially the same as those
adopted in such infill projects as the St Albans
scheme described earlier in this chapter, but to a
more intensive degree and without the crust of
existing frontage to hide its implications. With
Gehry's plan it could be said that the strategy of
back-land development has come out of the closet,
and is revealed to be, not an expedient form of
reinforcement to the existing pattern, but an
alternative to it, based upon a precise inversion of
each of its expected features. The recognition of
this inversion as an inherent characteristic of the
new urban mall, and not simply a side-effect of the
grosser redevelopment projects of the 1960s,
produces its own kind of shock:

Standing back a step or two, and looking at this kind of
urban solution from the point of view of the morphology of

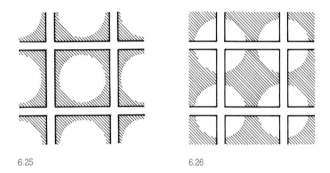

6.25   6.26

6.25 Diagram of pattern of frontage and value in
traditional street form (left).
6.26 Diagram of inverted pattern of frontage and value
resulting from redevelopment form adopted at Santa
Monica Place (right).

towns, we cannot fail to notice how commercialism and
functionalism have together managed to turn the city inside
out. Car-parking and merchandising, because they are the
most space-consuming and exacting elements determine
the 'city': the public functions are made subsidiary to the
great block of space and the citizens themselves, turned
into mere 'consumers', are ejected, to lie outside in
expectant subservience to the retailer. Something has gone
wrong somewhere.[4]

To analyse its implications it is indeed necessary to
consider the morphology of towns, and the ways in
which the morphology of the urban mall diverges
from it.

6.27 Santa Monica Place, Los Angeles: internal structure
bursting through block perimeter on Second Street.

Notes

1. When citizens in Philadelphia attempted to
demonstrate in The Gallery at Market East on an issue
of local politics they were prevented. They then held
a demonstration to protest at not being allowed to
demonstrate in a space partially funded by public
money. (Reported in Stephens, S., 1978:50).

2. See Sutcliffe, A., 1970.

3. From publicity brochure, 'Le Centre Commercial
Regional de la Part-Dieu'. Société des Centres
Commerciaux, Lyons.

4. Wright, L., in *The Architects' Journal*, 6 Nov.
1974:1090.

Chapter 7 The morphology of the urban mall

The problems of inversion and introversion in development patterns, and ambiguity in the character of public space created within them, are not unique to new shopping developments. It is a commonplace that the modern city as a whole exhibits a tendency to break down into specialised, single-use precincts – the university campus, the industrial estate, the leisure complex, the housing scheme for the young, for the old, for low-, middle- or upper-income ranges – each governed by internal, esoteric rules of development and implemented by specialist agencies whose terms of reference guarantee that they are familiar with other similar developments across the country, but know almost nothing of the dissimilar precincts which abut their own.

But retail development is perhaps the use most sensitive to the implications of these conditions for the city, since it provides the clearest manifestation of that elusive quality, 'life', which planners and citizens alike regard as the ultimate test of the urban environment. It does this because it is the one use which unequivocally requires and provides an open boundary between public and private space. Whereas other uses may puncture this boundary with openings, balancing their need for privacy with that for light and air and a greater or lesser desire to demonstrate that they have a social purpose, shopping altogether removes its function as a barrier. Instead it becomes a field for the maximum public exposure and display of the private functions within. Whereas the frontage of other uses obliquely signifies their public presence through detached advertisements and symbolic architectural devices, the shopping frontage *is* public presence made explicit and tangible. In a real sense it is a window, not just on the goods within, but upon the city itself. One goes window-shopping, but not window-working or window-playing, without inviting arrest.

In order to meet this desire of suburbanites to use 'their' shopping center outside of business hours, most of the larger centers have regulations which oblige tenants to keep their lights on until ten or eleven o'clock at night. In the majority of centers, this regulation also applies to Sundays and holidays. Northland and Eastland report that during favourable weather as many as 2000 cars are counted in the parking lots on Sundays and holidays.

(Gruen and Smith 1960:260)

The magnetism of frontage structures the private space on one side and the public on the other, and both are held in a balanced state of mutual opportunity and response from which the morphology of the shopping centre derives. The principles of this morphology, as discussed in Chapter 2, are both simple and capable of considerable variation. Consider, for example, the plan of the French suburban centre Rosny 2, to which reference was made earlier. Two department stores, Samaritaine to the north and BHV to the south, form the end magnets of a simple dumb-bell plan [2.23], between which a linear mall axis is tensioned. However, since they are some 280 metres apart, and hence beyond the normal spacing, the central zone of the axis is reinforced by a group of medium-sized units, of which the largest is a supermarket, Prisunic (La Redoute at the upper level). Side malls enter at each end and in the centre, to the upper mall level from the west side of the plan and to the lower level from the east. Around the basic configuration thus established, smaller units are now packed to take best advantage of the varying conditions which arise. At the points of focus, at each end and in the centre, the spacing of cross-walls narrows, as units compete for the most valuable frontage. The large units located in these positions require space, but proportionately less frontage, and small units crowd into their front zones to take advantage of this. While almost all of the people coming to the centre may be expected to pass these frontages, only one-sixth are likely to pass a unit with frontage only to a side mall, and these positions are thus occupied by secondary operations, such as banks, opticians, other service trades and a cinema, paying a lower rent per square metre. On the flank side-mall frontages of larger units facing the central mall, very small booths may be formed, perhaps only a metre deep, selling flowers, newspapers or books, to extract the last ounce of value from the available frontage.

The mall provides a public counterform to these private accommodations, establishing a hierarchy of spaces in both plan and section which corresponds to the levels of activity in each place. Narrow, single-height side malls lead to the broad, two-level central mall, which is articulated at its three points of focus by squares which connect the levels and, by their alignment, punctuate movement along the linear routes. The mall system thus essentially comprises node squares and route links, each of

which may occur in a variety of basic conditions. Node spaces for example may be associated with major magnet stores, or else with secondary concentrations of tenancies, with the first type usually acting as primary nodes and the second as subsidiary ones. In either case the node is also commonly located at the point of entry of a side mall. Similarly the routes tend to occur either as primary links, connecting node spaces and purely internal to the centre, or else as secondary ones, connecting the internal system to perimeter entrances.

To these elements a simple associational rule can be applied, from which the variety of mall structures can be derived. This rule, that primary nodes should be located no more than 200 metres apart, appears to have developed as a rule of thumb, frequently referred to in development literature[1] and is itself capable of some elaboration with respect to the disruption of additional secondary nodes, as will be seen.

From these simple premises the basic organisational structures of the mall system are generated. In the simplest multiple-node structure [7.1], two primary nodes, located next to end magnet stores and receiving incoming side-mall routes, are located 200 metres apart, with side malls, generally no more than 40 metres long, leading to entrance doors. This is the generic form of the Parly 2 [7.2] and Victoria Centre [7.3] plans, but these examples also indicate secondary features which tend to modify and elaborate this base structure. For although the 200-metre node spacing may be appropriate in terms of the movement of people within the main mall, it ignores the effect of secondary magnets elsewhere along the mall in differentiating its length, as occurs at the Victoria Centre, and also the need to introduce additional side-mall entries, or narrow their spacing, as occurs at Parly 2, both to increase accessibility from the car parks and to reduce travel distances for emergency escape out of the centre.[2] These factors tend to encourage the introduction of a side mall towards the centre of the plan, and with it a secondary node square located between the two primary end nodes, often associated with a secondary magnet.

This can be seen in a partial form at Fairview Mall [7.4], where although the primary node spacing does not 'require' a central square, central escalators and top lighting provide some emphasis in the middle of the plan near the entry of a side mall. At Brent Cross [7.5], and, as we have seen, at Rosny 2 [7.6], this central emphasis takes on the form of a fully articulated node square, in the latter case interrupting an otherwise over-extended primary node spacing.

The two-node diagram can be enlarged, in effect, by the growth of one of the side malls into a full mall [7.7], extending 200 metres to a third node and accompanying magnet. This forms the basis of the Yorkdale plan [7.8], which again exhibits the

7.1   Generic diagram of node structure for twin-magnet, or dumb-bell, shopping centre plan.

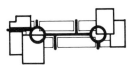

7.2   Parly 2: node structure diagram. 1 : 12,000.

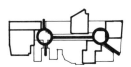

7.3   Victoria Centre: node structure diagram. 1 : 12,000.

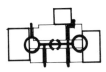

7.4   Fairview Mall: node structure diagram. 1 : 12,000.

7.5   Brent Cross: node structure diagram. 1 : 12,000.

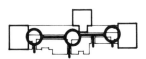

7.6   Rosny 2: node structure diagram. 1 : 12,000.

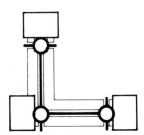

7.7   Generic diagram of node structure for triple-magnet shopping centre plan.

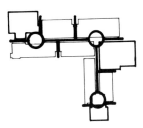

7.8   Yorkdale: node structure diagram. 1 : 12,000.

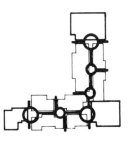

7.9   North Park: node structure diagram. 1 : 12,000.

7.10 Belle Epine: node structure diagram. 1 : 12,000.

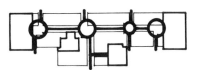

7.11 Creteil Soleil: node structure diagram. 1 : 12,000.

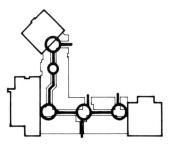

7.12 The Mall in Columbia: node structure diagram. 1 : 12,000.

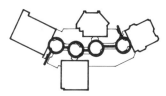

7.13 Northbrook Court: node structure diagram.
    1 : 12,000.

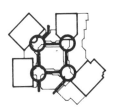

7.14 Scarborough Town Centre: node structure diagram.
    1 : 12,000.

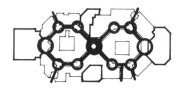

7.15 Sherway Gardens: node structure diagram.
    1 : 12,000.

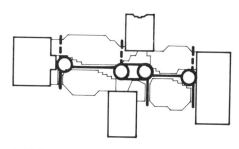

7.16 Santa Anita Fashion Park: node structure diagram.
    1 : 12,000.

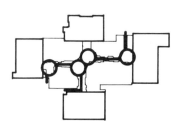

7.17 Eastridge: node structure diagram. 1 : 12,000.

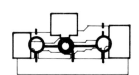

7.18 Fox Hills Mall: node structure diagram. 1 : 12,000.

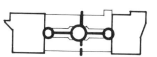

7.19 Oakville Place: node structure diagram. 1 : 12,000.

7.20 Galleria, White Plains: node structure diagram.
    1 : 12,000.

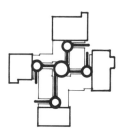

7.21 Lakehurst: node structure diagram. 1 : 12,000.

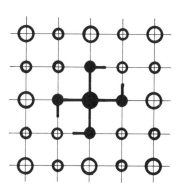

7.22 Lakehurst: node diagram as excerpt from general
    square grid.

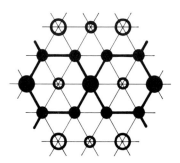

7.23 Sherway Gardens: node diagram as excerpt from
    general triangular grid.

symptoms of its subsequent elaboration, with side malls and intermediate magnet units located towards the middle of the main mall runs, though not yet acknowledged in its form as intermediate nodes. Such an acknowledgement occurs at North Park [7.9], where secondary squares are provided at each side-mall junction, breaking the main routes into two and three parts. The primary organisational structure is thus overlaid with a secondary one to build up a more elaborate sequence, or string, of nodes, the value and character of each of which will vary with its position in the overall pattern.

A great number of the centres which have been discussed earlier can be described in terms of the particular version of such a linear node string which they adopt, and which forms their underlying signature, or 'score'. Based upon a common interval of about 100 metres, with a variation of about plus or minus 30 metres, these strings set up increasingly elaborate and extended spatial and functional sequences. If we designate a primary magnet node with the letter A, and an intermediate node with b or B, depending on its significance in the plan, we begin with the simple primary node strings A–A (Parly 2, Victoria Centre) and A–A–A (Yorkdale) and then introduce intermediate nodes as A–b–A (Fairview Mall), A–B–A (Rosny 2, Brent Cross), A–B–A–b (Belle Epine [7.10]), A–A–b–A (Creteil Soleil [7.11]), A–B–A–b–A (The Mall in Columbia [7.12]), A–b–A–b–b–A (North Park), and so on. At Northbrook Court [7.13], where four magnet stores provide a high proportion of the lettable area, all four of the corresponding node squares are raised to equal status within a comparatively short mall length, creating a compressed A–A–A–A string. This forms a highly controlled sequence, with entries only at each end, and with the sculpture courts providing internally cross-referenced variations on a theme. At Scarborough [7.14], a similar four-node sequence is coiled into a circuit which can be entered at each corner, while at Sherway Gardens [7.15], the looping of a string in this way to create a continuous circuit is elaborated in figure-of-eight form, in which the centre node takes on a special significance in a route A–b–b–A'–b–b–A from end to end.

This tendency of the central node to assume a particular weight in the overall structure becomes especially marked in the later, 'department store', centres, in which a greater compression and unification of the plan was sought. Thus at Santa Anita [7.16], Eastridge [7.17] and Fox Hills Mall [7.18], the central space is enlarged, in the first two cases by the fusion of two magnet nodes, into a dominant element of the structure, in the form A–AA–A. Even in a simple dumb-bell plan of this later period, at Oakville Place [7.19], this centralising tendency is apparent, with side malls brought in to the plan at the midpoint, rather than the ends, and the formation of the most imposing

space at this point, to create a mall sequence a–B–a, effectively reversing the earlier, functional, definition of node dominance.

A similar pattern underlies the White Plains Galleria [7.20] but the pre-eminence of the central space is most apparent in the cruciform four-magnet plans such as that for Lakehurst [7.21], in which, with the completion of the fourth wing, a symmetrical pin-wheel mall form was envisaged. Each department store has its associated node square, centred about 160 metres apart across the cruciform, but because of the strongly centralised character of that form it is the central square, at the intersection of the four arms, which is clearly dominant, with the others appearing as dependent satellite spaces. The Lakehurst plan cannot be described in terms of a single linear string of nodes, but rather implies a grid, or net of node positions. Because of the restricted size of the centres in terms of the number of nodes they can develop, usually restricted to five or six, their plans hardly eloborate this possibility, although clearly a net-like node pattern would be feasible within the terms of the generating rules, either in a square form as at Lakehurst [7.22], or triangulated as at Sherway Gardens [7.23], with primary nodes at 200-metre centres and intermediate nodes between them.

These patterns may be taken as representing the 'deep structure' of the mall organisation, encapsulating features of circulation, spatial development and levels of economic activity, on which the variety of mall plans is built and from which their morphology derives. And if it were similarly possible to represent the organisation of the city as a whole in such a condensed form, one might then compare such characteristic organisational patterns of the mall and of its urban context, and thus identify any inherent structural differences and sources of conflict. Such an analysis might throw light on specific areas of difficulty, so that it would be possible to recognise whether, for example, the transformation of Main Street Buffalo arises from the conflict of two mutually incompatible patterns of organisation, or whether the problem is confined to treatment of the superstructure, as it were, so that, with suitable adjustments, such as the addition of external frontage as in the Eaton Centre facing Yonge Street, the new may be seen as an intensification of the old which may be successfully applied under conditions inferred from the structure itself.

Unfortunately no correspondingly abbreviated description of urban structure is readily available. Or rather, there are many such descriptions, each arising from some branch of the varied disciplines engaged in urban analysis, and none providing a universally accepted basis for the comparison sought here.

Some parallels to this shopping centre analysis are apparent in the early morphographic studies by German geographers of town plans in terms of their characteristic forms and patterns, as 'regular'

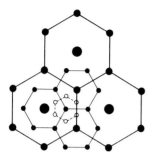

7.24 Diagram of market hierarchy according to Christaller's marketing theory.

and 'irregular' (Fritz 1894), 'spine-and-rib', 'ladder' and 'transitional' (Gradmann 1914) and so on. A more subtle appraisal was offered by the modern morphogenetic approach, pioneered by Conzen (1960) in his *Alnwick, Northumberland: A Study in Town-plan Analysis*, with its emphasis on the evolutionary nature of urban structure and its subdivision into 'morphological districts'. But although the insight provided by this method is invaluable in understanding the implications of change to a historic context, its emphasis upon past physical processes, and upon the plot, or burgage, as the fundamental unit of the structure, limits its ability to generate a general description of the urban context against which new patterns of organisation can be tested. Thus Whitehand (1981:17) has noted that: 'As Conzen makes clear . . . there is still no comprehensive theory of urban form capable of providing a basis for application to planning practice.'

The opposite objection could be raised to the frameworks devised by economic geographers, in which generalised structures are offered, but at a scale far removed from that of the local and physical events which characterise the developments with which we are concerned. Thus, although some analogy might be construed between the generic patterns of mall plans and those of classical central-place theory [*7.24*], with both related to the differentiation of levels of activity within their respective systems, the essentially regional scale of the latter, and its concentration upon purely economic, market factors, provides little guidance as to the structure of the city at the level of the district and quarter.

For consideration of the city at this scale we must turn to theories of urban design itself, the literature of which abounds with proposed structures and categories by which urban form may be understood. Again there is much in these theories which appears analogous to the considerations of mall form which we have examined. The method by which Camillo Sitte recommended that a city be planned, by the establishment of node elements, with magnet buildings (major public buildings in this case) facing squares embellished with fountains and monuments,

and linked together in patterns of locally appropriate variation, would be recognisable to any shopping centre developer. The two primary elements of Sitte's system, nodes and paths, were subsequently augmented by Kevin Lynch in his definition of the essential characteristics of urban form as paths, edges, nodes, districts and landmarks (Lynch 1960). Lynch (1960:119) recognised that the problem of defining the structure which relates these elements was a complex one: 'It is clear that the form of a city or of a metropolis will not exhibit some gigantic, stratified order. It will be a complicated pattern, continuous and whole, yet intricate and mobile.' Lynch declined to indicate any dimensional constraints relating his elements, such as we have suggested occurs in the retail examples, and there was a wide variation in the frequency with which elements occurred in the city analyses he provided.[3] Lynch thus concentrated on defining the qualities of the city 'image' rather than its structure, suggesting (1960:159) that 'It may turn out that some of these studies can in some way be quantified . . . but it seems likely that the core of the work will escape quantification, at least for some time, and that pattern and sequence considerations will be a primary direction' although we might eventually look forward (1960:118) 'toward a future synthesis of city form considered as a whole pattern'.

While subsequent urban designers have suggested alternative definitions of the essential urban ingredients,[4] and have extended Sitte's analysis of their possible characteristics,[5] few have proposed a syntax governing the relations of such a vocabulary, at least of a precision adequate to provide a methodical working structure.

One theorist who has done so is Christopher Alexander, whose 'Pattern Language' is both comprehensive and precise, defining both building and urban structures in terms of some 253 characteristic patterns, interrelated by a network of associations. Several of these patterns bear a resemblance to those discussed for retail malls, including, again, the principle of nodes and links as basic organising devices. Pattern 30 [*7.25*], describes 'Activity nodes' which '. . . must draw together the main paths in the surrounding community. The major pedestrian paths should converge on the square, with minor paths funnelling into the major ones, to create the basic star-shape of the pattern.' (Alexander *et al.* 1977:164) Alexander suggests that these nodes, which occur at the centres of 'Identifiable neighbourhoods' (Pattern 14), should be spaced about 300 metres apart, and be connected in string form by a dominant pedestrian route, or 'Promenade' (Pattern 31) [*7.26*], which would run down the centre of such a sequence of neighbourhoods so that each point in the community is within ten minutes' walking distance of it.

As with most urban design theories however, Alexander's patterns are prescriptive rather than

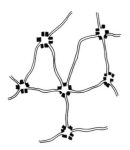

7.25 Pattern 30 from Alexander's *Pattern Language*.

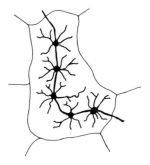

7.26 Pattern 31 from Alexander's *Pattern Language*.

descriptive, specifying how the city ought to be, rather than how it actually is. For the purposes of trying to relate the characteristic structure of the retail mall to that of its urban context, neither the urban geographers' models of how the latter has arisen in the past, nor the urban designers' proposals as to how it might best be clarified in the future, thus provide an entirely appropriate framework, although both contain suggestive parallels with the retail forms.

These parallels are pervasive and occur on a variety of levels. We have already seen the way in which the appeal of many specialty centres lies in the way in which they mimic or reproduce an image of the city in history, while the characteristics of its key element, the street, with all its overtones of social theatre and public purpose, are evoked in a wide range of retail projects. Indeed it could be argued that whereas the smaller scale of the nineteenth-century arcade suggested references to specific building types within the city, such as the cathedral (Mengoni designed the circumference of the glass dome of the Galleria Vittorio Emanuele II to coincide with that of the dome of St Peter's in Rome[6]), the implicit model for larger-scale shopping centre projects in this century has been the city itself.

This notion may seem absurd and paradoxical. After all, it is the anti-urban and insular character of the modern shopping centre which raises the whole question of its relationship to the city. And if such references to urban patterns and components can indeed be recognised in retail forms, it is apparent that they amount to a highly

selective reading of the city as a model, at least as it appears today. To understand the basis of this selection, and hence the motives for these references, it is necessary to acknowledge one dominant factor in the evolution of new shopping forms as they have occurred since the eighteenth century. This lies in their response to the problem of circulation, and above all of pedestrian circulation, in the increasingly congested conditions of the modern city. The creation of sidewalks, of colonnaded pavements, of arcades and of department stores, were all attempts to define discrete areas of pedestrian circulation free from the hazards of wheeled traffic, which, long before the invention of the internal combustion engine, had become a major obstacle to movement on foot.[7] As these pedestrian spaces, essential for shopping, became extended into the precincts, malls and pedestrian zones of recent years, so they developed a private architectural language appropriate to their specific condition – a language based upon that of the city, but the city as a pedestrian place. And the more isolated, the more independent they became of the mass of the actual city by virtue of its increasingly elaborate systems of wheeled transportation, the more intensively were they obliged to articulate the language of the pedestrian city within their own boundaries. Thus, with a fine irony, the out-of-town regional shopping centre, commonly regarded as the development form most hostile to the traditional city, has adopted all of the characteristic symbolism and iconography of that paradigm of traditional urbanism, the medieval hill-town, with its sequence of landmark elements signifying its presence in the landscape [*7.27; 7.28*], defensive walled enclosure [*7.29; 7.30*], monumental gateways [*7.31; 7.32*], sheltered internal streets [*7.33; 7.34*] and node piazzas with fountains and major functions [*7.35; 7.36*].

If these correspondences may then be seen, not simply as historicist games nor merely as tricks of visual merchandising, but as a necessary attempt to order an isolated pedestrian world, we might ask whether the organisational structures of extended retail mall systems also represent a selective version of the characteristic structures of the pedestrian city. Whether, that is, within the restrictions of their topographical and functional simplicity, their acknowledgement of the patterns of pedestrian movement and of pedestrian tolerance of distance might make it possible to regard them as special cases of more general urban patterns in which pedestrian circulation is paramount.

Certainly it is possible to identify such patterns in the formation of towns before the Industrial Revolution, although whether they provide a general morphological description of such towns is a question which lies beyond the scope of this study.[8] In terms of their administration by districts and parishes, for example, the scale of subdivision of medieval cities into units dominated by central

7.27–7.36 The iconography of the pedestrian city.

7.27 Markers in the landscape: San Gimignano, Italy.

7.30 Definition of perimeter: Park Place, Las Vegas.

7.28 Markers in the landscape: Park Place, Las Vegas.

7.31 Entrance gateway: Wurzburger Tor, Rothenburg, Germany.

7.29 Definition of perimeter: city walls of Rothenburg, Germany.

7.32 Entrance gateway: The Fashion Show, Las Vegas.

7.33 Sheltered internal routes: Bergamo, Italy.

7.36 Focal spaces: Central Square, Eastridge Center, San Jose.

7.34 Sheltered internal routes: Sherway Gardens, Toronto.

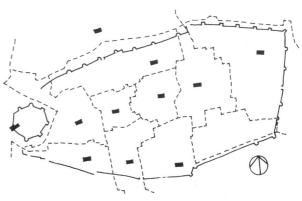

7.37 Diagram of parish boundaries with city churches in medieval Oxford. 1 : 12,000.

7.35 Focal spaces: Piazza della Cisterna, San Gimignano, Italy.

'magnet' functions was often analogous to that of the retail forms, as in the case of medieval Oxford [7.37], whose parish churches formed the foci of a parochial subdivision of the walled town into areas averaging about 4 hectares, that is of about 100 metres radius around each church. The basic cell of this organisation can be seen in isolation in rural settlements, transitional between individual farmsteads and small villages, and vividly at Monteriggioni in central Italy [7.38], where a fortified wall, 200 metres in diameter, contains buildings clustered around a central square from which streets lead to east and west gates.

From this unit a great variety of organisational patterns could be constructed, adapted to the topographical, social and historical circumstances of each case, but broadly informed by a physical interval of about 200 metres (or one furlong, the common standard of land measure) between points

117

7.38 Monteriggioni: aerial view.

7.40 Rottweil: node structure diagram. 1 : 12,000.

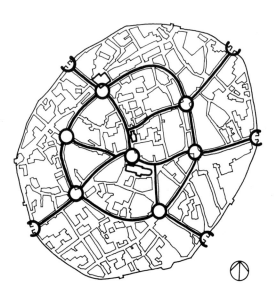

7.39 Nördlingen: node structure diagram. 1 : 12,000.

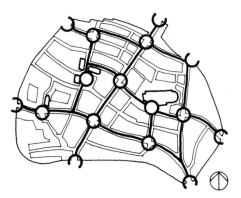

7.41 Freiburg: node structure diagram. 1 : 12,000.

of focus. Where topography allowed, these patterns often approximated to the square or triangulated nets which the geometry of a regular interval implies. Thus at Nördlingen and Soest in Germany, for example, the progressive enlargements of the towns by the successive construction of circular city walls at 200, 400 and finally, in the case of Soest, 600 metres from the centre, built up structures which, for all their irregularity and complexity of detailed plot form, established node positions for public buildings and spaces in arrangements broadly conforming to those of a triangulated net [7.39]. The orthogonal net is most clearly visible in the 'planned' foundations as in the *bastide* and Zähringer towns. Of the latter, Rottweil [7.40], Villingen and Freiburg [7.41], in south-west Germany illustrate the progressive development of such a pattern from a simple cruciform plan into a larger net form.

For most settlements of this period however, irregular topography, disjointed phases of development, and the presence of major routes passing through the town, all tended to disturb such homogeneous patterns. A common result of these disturbances was the development of a

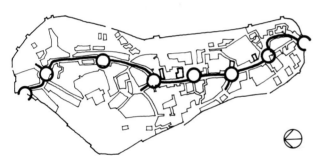

7.42 Spello: node structure diagram. 1 : 12,000.

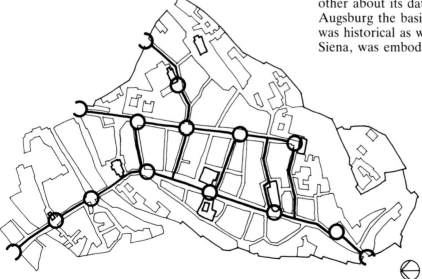

7.43 Landshut: node structure diagram. 1 : 12,000.

dominant string of nodes within the structure, acting as a spine of primary functions around which secondary zones would be arranged. In the case of many Italian towns, built on steeply sloping sites, the plan consisted of little more than one such meandering string, along which major public buildings and their associated piazzas were arranged. This occurred for example at Spello [7.42] and Montepulciano, built along steep promontory-like ridges, and across the saddle-back ridge of Urbino. A second string might then develop alongside the first, to create the 'ladder' arrangement identified by Gradmann, and elegantly demonstrated at Landshut in Bavaria [7.43], where the principal public buildings established a dominant string along Altstadt [7.44], which was complemented by secondary functions along the parallel Neustadt. Again, a third parallel string might be laid down on a predominantly linear site of sufficient width, as at Heidelberg [7.45] and Orvietto.

On steeply sloping hillside sites, the even net of the notional node pattern tended to be compressed down the line of slope to create the stretched grid form visible in a number of plans, such as those of Gubbio and Assisi. Moreover, discontinuities of topography or stages of development often had the effect of breaking the net down into distinct zones, or morphological districts, each tailored to their specific conditions. Thus many of the larger medieval towns have the character of assemblages of net fragments, tied together by a system of dominant strings. At Siena [7.46], the topographical basis of this subdivision is apparent in the growth of the city in the form of three linear districts along the three ridges dominating its site, and whose spine routes met in the centre of the plan at the Croce di Travaglio. These routes then acted as the main frame from which the major urban elements, the Campo and the Cathedral Square for example, were, as it were, suspended, counterbalancing each other about its datum like elements in a mobile. At Augsburg the basis of the morphological districts was historical as well as topographical and, as at Siena, was embodied in the political and social subdivision of the city (Bischofstadt, Obere Stadt, Untere Stadt, Jakober-Vorstadt).

Two further features of these city structures are of interest in connection with the characteristic mall arrangements discussed earlier. The first concerns the treatment and relative weight of the central point in the overall structure. As in the shopping centre plans, this varied greatly from case to case, but it is notable that where the central place was required to resolve a number of incoming routes, it often adopted an extended bi-nodal form similar to

that seen at Eastridge and Santa Anita. Thus at Todi and Perugia, for example, where the plans were broken down by irregular topography into miscellaneous morphological districts, the string elements dominating each were locked together at the central point by a bi-nodal central place of this form [7.47]. The second feature worth noting is the tendency of secondary intermediate node positions to develop within the overall structure as the density of development increased. At Rottweil, for example, this secondary pattern is neatly delineated by the locations of wells and fountains set out within the plan, at which point later public buildings were established [7.48], and a similar intensification of the development pattern can be seen in the disposition of smaller churches and *palazzi* in a number of the towns.

If then it may be possible to see in the apparently random and picturesque plans of medieval towns certain basic development patterns and features which appear to be analogous to those operating in modern mall plans, it must be said that these hardly provide an inevitable and deterministic basis for their generation from fixed 'rules'. Rather these rules may be said to have set out a pattern of possibilities for prime site locations and connecting routes based upon the limitations of pedestrian movement. In each case the character of the city arose from the way in which the game was played, and the most memorable parts of pedestrian cities result from the successive elaboration and development of the pattern, generation after generation, to manipulate its characteristics.

If there is one city which above all others ought to illustrate the principles of a pedestrian-based structure it is surely Venice, and since it has also been cited as the inspiration of such divergent modern planning concepts as Clarence Perry's suburban neighbourhood unit (by Lewis Mumford 1961:369) and Le Corbusier's 1933 plan for a new city on the left bank of the Scheldt at Antwerp (by Le Corbusier himself, 1967:269), it is worth referring to it here. For in the case of Venice the formation of a pedestrian city by the accretion of Monteriggioni-like cells, which has been inferred

7.44 Landshut: view south along Altstadt with spire of St Martinskirche marking one of sequence of node places along the length of the street.

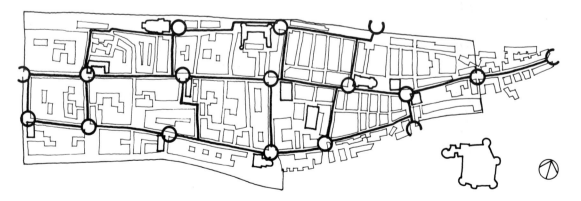

7.45 Heidelberg: node structure diagram. 1 : 12,000.

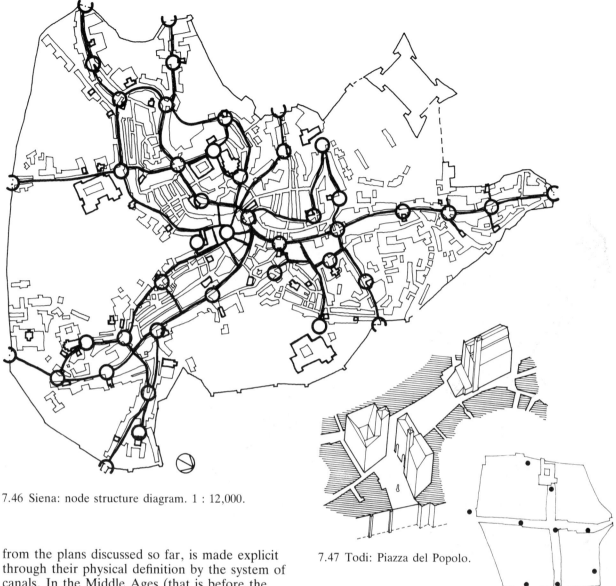

7.46 Siena: node structure diagram. 1 : 12,000.

7.47 Todi: Piazza del Popolo.

7.48 Rottweil: development of secondary nodes.
1 : 12,000 (right).

from the plans discussed so far, is made explicit through their physical definition by the system of canals. In the Middle Ages (that is before the enlargement of the zones around the Arsenale and Nuova Piazza d'Armi in the east and the Stazione Marittima and Stazione della Strada Ferrata in the west) the 103 island units of the main Rialto group amounted to some 350 hectares. Although they varied considerably in size and in the extent of their development, a typical unit was thus equivalent in area to a square 185 metres wide, with a central node space and church, and linked by bridges across the bounding canals to adjacent units to form a net structure, warped and inflected by the meander of the Grand Canal [7.49].

Now in translating the Venetian pattern into a modern planning principle, both Perry, interpreting it in terms of 400-metre-radius neighbourhoods, and Le Corbusier, in terms of 400-metre-square highway superblocks, ignored this physical structure. Concentrating on its system of traffic segregation, they isolated that feature as a metaphor for forms of modern development, freely adapting its scale to suit preferred notions of

community or infrastructure. As a model of a wholly pedestrian organisation for a city, however, it was precisely its scale, and the introverted (in relation to the canal service corridors) pattern of centric development units based on node foci, which were characteristic. And in terms of the urban mall, it is precisely those features which make the city such a tantalising, and some would say dangerous, model for modern urban development.

The period which separates us from these medieval examples of pedestrian city form is marked not only by the development of modern transportation systems, but also by a protracted programme of rationalisation of its inherent features, of which Perry's and Le Corbusier's studies are but late examples. This programme,

121

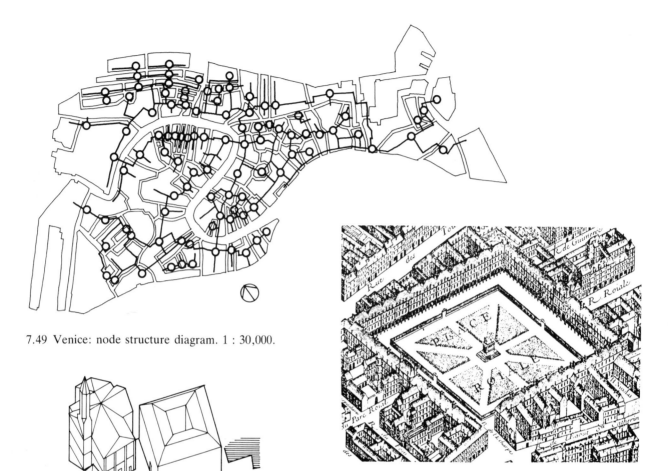

7.49 Venice: node structure diagram. 1 : 30,000.

7.50 Pienza: central square.

7.51 Place Royale, Paris.

beginning with the first tentative Renaissance co-ordinated planning projects, and culminating in the simplified and infinitely extensible grid plans by which industrial cities and new territories were colonised in the nineteenth century, effectively defined the context within which the modern urban mall must operate, and requires some brief comment here.

It would be possible to regard Renaissance urbanism in this light, as a programme, not so much to rediscover the city of classical antiquity, as to analyse and reconstruct the elements of the medieval city in the light of the classical tradition. Each of the generic elements – the node, the string and the net – might then be isolated and resolved as an independent design component – the piazza, the *via triomphalis* and the rational grid – and reassembled to comprise the ideal city. In each case

the progress of that study led towards an increasing simplification of the element, as its form approximated more and more closely to the geometric abstraction which could be inferred from its place within the medieval structure. As regards the node element, for example, this process is graphically illustrated by two projects, separated by 150 years. In the first, Rosselino's design for the main square of Pienza, of 1459–62, the centre of a small medieval town, little more than one main street, about 350 metres long, running along the ridge of a hill, was reconstructed with the erection of four new buildings around a small piazza [*7.50*]. With loggia, pilastered walls and gridded pavement, these buildings contrived a monumental focus for the town, resolving the irregular street alignment on each side by their asymmetrical disposition about the axis of the central building, the cathedral, and relating the datum of the square to the surrounding countryside through long views created down its flanks. This kind of solution, idealised in its references but contingent in its formal response to the particular circumstances of the city and its topography, contrasts with that of the second project, the Place Royale (Place des Vosges) in Paris [*7.51*], in which the components were assembled to create a regular square form.

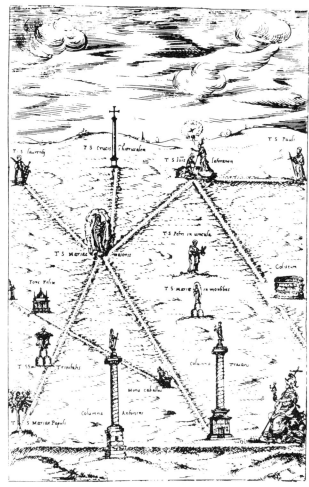

7.52 Sixtus V's node structure diagram of Rome.

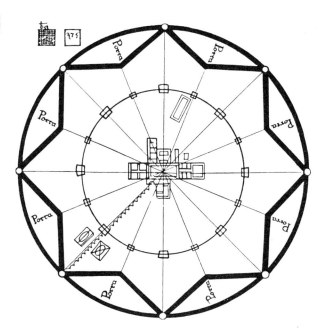

7.53 Antonio Filarete's plan for Sforzinda.

7.54 L'Enfant's plan for Washington DC.

Together with the triangular Place Dauphine and circular Place des Victoires, the Place Royale provided a platonic distillation of the medieval node space, reproducible and geometrically exact.

A similar progression can be seen in the development of increasingly abstract versions of the string and net structures of the pedestrian city throughout this period, in the monumental axial systems of Sixtus V [7.52] and baroque planning in the case of the former, and in the studies for ideal city plans in the case of the latter. Such plans initially retained the function of the net as an ordering system for node elements throughout the city, as in Filarete's Sforzinda [7.53], in which the disposition of squares and streets represented an idealised version of the medieval plans of Nördlingen and Soest. Increasingly, however, they became concerned purely with the rationalisation of circulation and plot subdivision and the corresponding suppression of any sense of local hierarchy of functional organisation within the universal grid, until, in their application to the planning of new settlements in North America, the articulation of the street grid by public spaces could be regarded as a question of local preference (as in Penn's plan for Philadelphia) rather than as

an intrinsic feature of the system. The end-product of this process of abstraction can be seen in L'Enfant's plan for Washington DC [7.54], in which the structural features of the medieval city have become autonomous systems, layered one upon the other. The net, now reduced to the orthogonal grid of city blocks and orientated to the cardinal points, becomes a neutral field upon which an independent system of monumental strings is disposed, its nodes sublimated into symbolic objects representing the institutions of the new republic.

The implications of this transformation of the organising structure of the city from a parochial, cellular and pedestrian-scaled pattern into a route-dominated system are vividly illustrated in the eight plans submitted for the rebuilding of London in

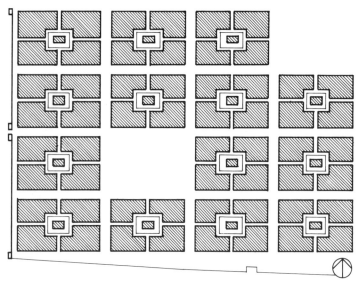

7.55 South-west quarter of Newcourt's plan of London.
   1 : 12,000.

1666. The best known of these, by Wren and Evelyn, adopted the patterns of Continental baroque planning, being in effect extended string structures based on 'free' nodes which, particularly in the latter case, display every conceivable geometric node space variation. The plan offered by Valentine Knight was, by contrast, a straight grid plan of the future North American pattern, while Robert Hooke's added four major public spaces to such a grid, in form similar to those proposed for Philadelphia. All of these schemes represented variations of 'modern' route-based planning organisations, in which the city is represented as a hatched ground, penetrated by arteries articulated to a greater or lesser degree by public spaces[9]. One project, however, offered a radically different interpretation of the rationalised city plan, and one which retained the functional significance of the medieval node arrangement in the structure. This was the proposal by Richard Newcourt who, of all the competitors, was most familiar with the detailed structure of the medieval city which had been destroyed in the September Great Fire, having surveyed it and published the result as *An Exact Delineation of the Cities of London and Westminster*, in 1658. Newcourt's plan [7.55] reformulated this medieval structure, with its fuzzy edges and irregular conditions, in the pristine Cartesian vocabulary of his age, creating a matrix of identical parish units, 260 × 174 metres (or 260 × 238 metres in a second version) across, each with its central square and church approached by four streets penetrating the unit from the surrounding thoroughfares from which it could be closed off at night by gates.

Newcourt's plan thus inverted the gradations of social and economic value implicit in the other London plans, locating foci at the centre, rather than the edges, of blocks of development, and providing an abstract model of the medieval organisation of Venice on the one hand, and of the modern urban mall on the other. Though realised only once, in Ogelthorpe's plan for Savannah, Georgia, some sixty-seven years later (based upon ward units 206 metres square), it remained a potent alternative interpretation of urban structure, and one which awaited the need for a pedestrian-dominated network in the city for its time to come.

Notes

1. For example:

   'The ideal mall length is considered to be in the order of 400 to 600 feet.' (*Shopping for Pleasure* 1969:19)

   'Without doubt one of the simplest and most effective designs is the 'dumbell' layout. This is only really effective so long as the Mall length can be kept to a length of about 600 feet.' (*Design for Shopping* 1970:16)

   'Mall lengths were of the order of 600–800 feet before a break was injected in the form of a central feature.' (*Shopping Around* 1972)

   'Experience has shown that there is a maximum distance of about 200–250 metres (600–800 feet) which shoppers are prepared to travel from one focal point to another. If distances are greater than this, they tend to lose interest and fail to complete the journey.' (Northen and Haskoll 1977:40)

2. In the UK the government publication *Fire Precautions in Town Centre Development* (1972), Fire Prevention Guide No. 1, HMSO London, recommended that the maximum distance from one mall exit to another measured along the mall should not exceed 90 metres (p. 17).

3. Lynch identified 17 'nodes' in the central area of Boston, within an area of about 950 hectares, and only 2 in downtown Los Angeles, with an area of 500 hectares. The proportion of 'landmarks' for the 2 cities was reversed, however, with 30 in the first and 32 in the second (Lynch 1960)

4. For example, the four 'conditions' proposed by Jane Jacobs, as 'the need for mixed primary uses'; 'the need for small blocks'; 'the need for aged buildings'; 'the need for concentration' (Jacobs 1961). Closer in nature to Lynch's elements, Charles Moore has suggested place, path, pattern and edge' (Bloomer and Moore 1977), and Christian Norberg-Schulz 'Place and Node : Path and Axis : Domain and District' (Norberg-Schulz 1971).

5. For example, the analysis of the forms of city squares by Rob Krier (1979).

6. The imagery of Mengoni's plan is discussed in Geist (1983:384).

7. Geist (1983) provides a graphic description of the impact of the development of fast horse-drawn carriages on the cities of the seventeenth and eighteenth centuries.

8. This question is discussed more fully in Maitland, B. S., 'A Minimal Urban Structure' unpublished Ph.D. Thesis, University of Sheffield, 1982.

9. See Reps (1965) for a discussion of the attempts to integrate public spaces into the grid plans of the United States.

Chapter 8 The generator of new city patterns

If this interpretation of the historical development of urban structure generated by consideration of circulation and functional organisation has any validity, it may serve as some sort of critical framework within which we might examine the recent emergence of novel forms of development. For it suggests that the underlying organisational structure of the new urban malls is not simply an extension of the existing urban framework, but rather represents an alternative, mirror-image principle of development; that this structure can be seen to have precedents in more archaic and essentially pedestrian, urban formations, whose patterns were superseded by the rationalised, route-dominated forms of Renaissance planning and the Industrial Revolution; and that the characteristic features of inversion, of concentration of value in the centre of the block, and relegation of its periphery to secondary service functions, are not marginal side-effects of mall enclosure, but are inherent features of the new structure. In considering these mall plans, it is as if we were witnessing the subversion of the classical city of Wren or, more likely, Valentine Knight, by the growth within it of Newcourt's parochial cells. Burrowing through the hard frontages of its blocks, they use it as a shell, within which they excavate their node places. The openings they offer to the existing streets are essentially sacrificial and conciliatory until such time as neighbouring blocks have been similarly colonised and a net can be established between them, drawing all primary frontage into the new system.

The colonising character of these developments is most apparent in those projects which have been carried out within city blocks of strong existing frontage, and particularly that of a historical or otherwise sensitive nature, in which, as we have seen in a number of English examples, the strategy of back-land development is permitted as acceptable intensification which ensures the renewal of the existing fabric. To cite an American case, the NewMarket specialty centre in the historic Society Hill area of Philadelphia, Pennsylvania [8.1], clearly states the relationship of old and new parts, in which the latter, clad in a system of glazed cubes [8.2], resides, like some kind of crystalline hermit crab, within the protective carapace of existing brick row-houses, infilled as necessary to complete the perimeter.

However, this mutually tolerant and beneficial relationship could hardly be supported in the more intensive conditions of the central business district, under which the inherent logic of the new pattern, and the physical form of its component parts, gradually unfolded within the context, not only of greater densities of development, but also of other superimposed site uses.

At first the pattern appeared as a marginal adjunct to such uses, generally office developments, in which, as at Place Ville Marie in Montreal [8.3], and the Toronto-Dominion Centre in Toronto [8.4], a podium shopping layer was incorporated at the foot of office towers. Although modest in form, these malls demonstrated two distinctive features which were to be characteristic of the more elaborate solutions which followed. The first of these was the importance to the system of the vertical cores serving development above and which created points of concentration of pedestrian movement deep within the site block. At Place Ville Marie for example, the largest of the office towers over the podium, the forty-five-storey cruciform plan Royal Bank of Canada Building, provided about 0.4 hectare of floor space at each of its levels, so that the point at which its central elevator banks met the ground represented, in effect, the circulation focus of some 45 acres (18 hectares) of intensive city development, and a prime generator of movement within the podium malls.

The second feature which they exhibited was the displacement of the pedestrian circulation datum in relation to that of the surrounding city. In both examples this occurred as a corollary of relating the level of the podium roof plaza to the adjoining street level, so that the mall system was sunk below it. Although this appeared to offer a considerable increase to the system of pedestrian space at street level [8.5], this gain was more nominal than real, since, for most of the time, the greatest pedestrian activity occurred in the sheltered routes, with shopping frontage, below the plaza. The resulting impression of a shear fault around the perimeter of the site, by which the strata within it have been displaced in relation to its surroundings was most graphically evinced in another 1960s development, built a few blocks to the south of Place Ville Marie, at Place Bonaventure, in which the opposite kind of displacement seemed to have occurred. For instead of sinking into the site, it was as if the basement levels of a city block had here been pulled bodily out of the ground [8.6], revealing

8.1 NewMarket, Philadelphia: axonometic sketch of development.

8.2 NewMarket, Philadelphia: view of central court.

their massive retaining walls as an external shell to the introspective functions within. This impression was reinforced by the organisational pattern of the development, which was based on a ring of perimeter cores surrounding the 'soft' centre, rather than on isolated tower cores as in the other two cases [8.7].

127

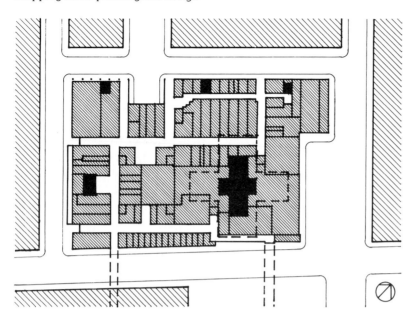

8.3   Place Ville Marie, Montreal: plan at basement
concourse level. 1 : 3,000.

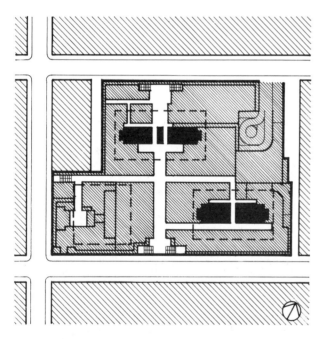

8.4   Toronto-Dominion Centre, Toronto: plan at
basement concourse level. 1 : 3,000.

In each of these examples the shopping element
was a relatively minor feature of the development,
and its mall system little more than corridors
between entrances and circulation cores. At Place
Bonaventure an escalator well linking two shopping
levels, and at Place Ville Marie a sunken courtyard
connecting the upper plaza to the podium routes,
began to suggest the formation of a node space in
the centre of the plan, independent of the
circulation cores, but these were still marginal
articulations. Numerous variations of the 'sunken

court in the podium' arrangement were attempted,
as in the Manulife Centre in Toronto [8.8], in
which it acted as a transitional outdoor area,
belonging fully to neither street nor mall system.
Eventually, however, it became absorbed into the
latter and, transformed now into an atrium space,
provided the focal element by which that system
might establish its full autonomy.

This shift may be seen at Broadway Plaza in
downtown Los Angeles, in which the space was, in
effect, a forecourt standing in front of The
Broadway department store, which occupied half of
the block, and between two tower buildings, the
Hyatt Regency Hotel and the 700 office building
[8.9]. Roofed over, however, and excavated out to
connect to a lower shopping level, it became the
central hall of the development [8.10], to which the
circulation cores of the surrounding elements
directly connected. Visitors arriving by car parked
on two levels of parking below the department
store and six levels above it, and thence were
brought into the central hall towards which the
hotel and office lobbies orientated themselves,
retaining private entrances to the street for taxi and
coach arrivals. The presence of a strong department
store element in this project raises parallels with
out-of-town centre forms, and these are most
vividly evoked in the Water Tower Place
development in Chicago, which similarly filled a
city block and contained not one, but two,
department stores, which established a highly
compressed dumb-bell plan seven storeys deep
[8.11]. Both department stores, Lord and Taylor,
and Marshall Field, retained frontage at ground
level facing Michigan Avenue, but the displacement
of the pedestrian datum inherent in the
arrangement was dramatically announced at the

8.5 Place Ville Marie, Montreal: view of open plaza.

8.6 Place Bonaventure, Montreal: view of north elevation to Lagauchetiere Street.

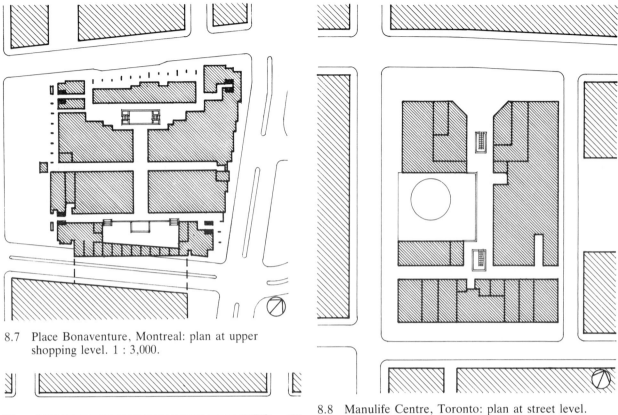

8.7 Place Bonaventure, Montreal: plan at upper shopping level. 1 : 3,000.

8.8 Manulife Centre, Toronto: plan at street level. 1 : 3,000.

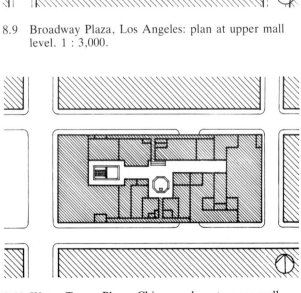

8.9 Broadway Plaza, Los Angeles: plan at upper mall level. 1 : 3,000.

8.11 Water Tower Place, Chicago: plan at upper mall level. 1 : 3,000.

8.10 Broadway Plaza, Los Angeles: view of central space.

main entrance to the centre from the street, where escalators flanked by cascading pools and planters, projected forward between the department store frontages. The escalators led up to the first level of the mall [8.12], which connected the department stores, intermediate shops and, at the far corner, cinemas and the core of a seventy-four-storey hotel and apartment tower. The dumb-bell mall plan was repeated on the shopping levels above, the whole arrangement pinned together by a well rising through the superimposed central squares, and containing three glass lifts [8.13].

With this scheme the central space emerged as the dominant focus of the plan, around which the accommodation was densely packed and contained within the taut blank envelope of a gridded cube built up to the plot boundaries [8.14]. A somewhat bizarre variant of this form was provided at the Citicorp Center in Manhattan in which the sunken forecourt reappeared as the apparent outcome of some major disaster which had demolished most of the bottom ten storeys of a 280-metre-high office tower [8.15], behind which an atrium rose through the seven storeys of office and shopping development which filled the eastern two-thirds of the block [8.16]. The central space in this case was ringed by galleries [8.17], on to which the three floors of shopping – The Market at Citicorp – faced, and provided the setting for jazz concerts,

recitals, fashion shows and all of the other events customarily associated with out-of-town malls.

The transformation of the mall square into an atrium space was a critical step in the development of the new pattern, since it provided the means of integrating non-retail uses into its schema. The advantages of adding non-retail uses to shopping developments had long been argued by the architects of out-of-town centres, who had recognised the social and economic advantages which could accrue. In the 1950s Gruen had urged developers to 'acquire all of the commercially or industrially zoned land, and/or potentially zoned land' (Gruen and Smith 1960:105) around a new centre site, in order to preclude competitive retail elements, take advantage of increased land values engendered by the magnetism of the new centre, and create a balanced mix of uses attracted by it. But although sites for offices, banks, hotels, medical centres or apartment blocks were often planned by centre developers around the periphery of the shopping centre car park, they shied away from a more comprehensive integration, preferring to concentrate on the single use towards which their experience, funding, letting and management arrangements were directed. And, with a few notable exceptions such as Pelli's early project for the Santa Anita centre, the form of the out-of-town centres implicitly recognised this exclusivity, indicating in their closed-ended plans no way in which other uses might relate to the mall structure. Only in their latest stages of development, under pressure of more restricted site opportunities, have plans for American out-of-town centres belatedly appeared in which an equal bulk of non-retail uses is seen as part of an overall development strategy, as in Gruen's project for the Park Meadows Town Center outside Denver, Colorado [8.18], in which a five-magnet linear mall forms the conclusion to an axial arrangement of linked office atria and hotel and leisure uses.

In the more intensive conditions of the city centre, however, the exclusive dedication of a site to a single use could hardly apply, and high land costs necessarily entailed the layering of other functions on top of shopping levels. The vertical divisions of this arrangement might assume quite independent forms, as in the tower and podium solutions we have discussed, with only the vertical circulation cores providing points of connection. But with the introduction of the atrium, an organisational pattern became available for a wide variety of central area uses which related directly to that of the shopping levels below, and made possible a vertical integration of functions equivalent to the horizontal integration initiated by the mall net.

Appropriately enough, the history of the atrium corresponded closely to that of the mall arcade, undergoing a period of invention and development in the nineteenth century, followed by almost complete neglect in the first half of the twentieth.[1]

8.12 Water Tower Place, Chicago: view of escalators connecting street level up to first mall level.

8.13 Water Tower Place, Chicago: view of glass elevator
bank rising through shopping levels in central space.

8.14 Water Tower Place, Chicago: view of west elevation
to Michigan Avenue.

8.15 Citicorp, New York: view of tower raised above open plaza on Lexington Avenue frontage.

8.17 Citicorp, New York: view of central atrium in the Market.

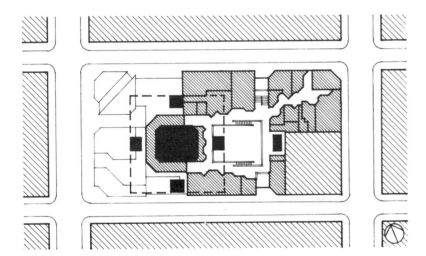

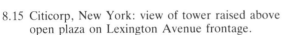

8.16 Citicorp, New York: plan at upper mall level.
1 : 3,000.

As an equivalent form-type, glazing over the courtyard rather than the street, it appeared as the entrance lobby of Victorian hotels, such as the Brown Palace Hotel in Denver, and as the central well of office buildings such as Burnham and Roots' Rookery Building in Chicago. Bringing light into the centre of a deep block plan, it came into its own as a dramatic internal visual compensation for buildings with poor outlook, as in the case of

Frank Lloyd Wright's Larkin Building, located in a coal yard. As that example also demonstrated, it permitted the treatment of the whole building block as a single managed environment, with minimal external envelope. In this respect it again acted in a manner parallel to that of the mall in shopping developments, for as traffic noise and considerations of heat loss and solar gain tended to reduce the required openings in the external

133

8.18 Park Meadows, Denver, Colorado: rendering of proposed mixed-use development. (Courtesy Gruen Associates)

8.19 The Galleria, Houston: view of atrium forming focus of second phase.

8.20 Bonaventure Center, Los Angeles: view of central atrium, with shopping levels around perimeter facing in to hotel lounge seating pods suspended in the centre.

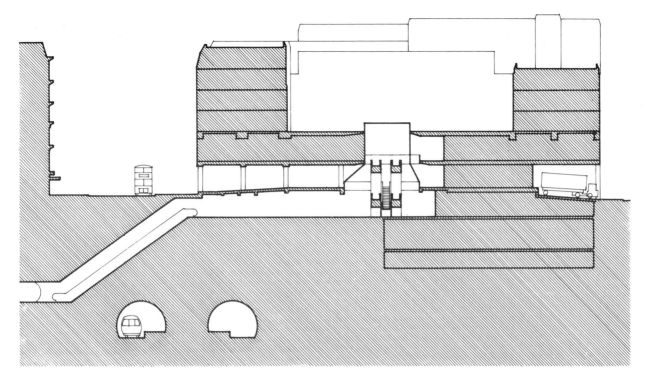

8.21 West One, London: section through development.
1 : 600.

envelope of buildings, so they were able to increase
their openness towards the central atrium, which
acted as a plenum or intermediate volume between
private space and the exterior. These environmental
factors, coupled with analyses of effective site
development patterns exemplified by the studies
carried out by the Martin Centre at Cambridge,
formerly the Centre for Land Use and Built Form
Studies, which demonstrated the fallacy of assumed
development gains for high tower forms, provided a
powerful argument for the rediscovery of the
atrium as the focus of relatively low-rise, densely
packed and introspective urban forms appropriate
to a wide range of uses. In relation to the
pedestrian net generated by shopping, it provided
the vital central node element, specific in form, but
non-specific in function, which the malls of Place
Ville Marie and the Toronto-Dominion Center had
lacked, and thus created the circumstances for the
definitive reformulation of Newcourt's parochial
structure in the modern city.

The precise sectional organisation by which
shopping and other uses could be arranged around
the atrium space was capable of considerable
variation. In the second phase of the Houston
Galleria for example, the square plan and central
escalator well of the Neiman-Marcus department
store which closed one end of the first phase, was
expanded into a full atrium form in which layers of
offices and car parking sandwiched two floors of
shopping which extended out from the linear first-
phase mall. Elevator banks were located in the

centre of the atrium space, with bridges connecting
across to each of the thirteen floor levels served
[8.19]. Again, as at the Bonaventure Center in Los
Angeles, the upper levels of accommodation might
be located on top of the atrium, in that case in the
form of the cylindrical Bonaventure Hotel which
has, as it were, been pulled vertically out of the
city block below, leaving a void ringed by five
levels of small specialty shops which face across to
the pods and galleries of hotel lounges which are
suspended in the central space around the
circulation cores [8.20].

The vertical elaboration of shopping levels about
the central space was further induced in those cases
where development coincided with an underground
rail station, where the existence of a strong
pedestrian generator below ground, coupled with
new development above ground, weakened the
already tenuous dominance of street level as the
implicit datum of the resulting system of
movement. Thus in two such projects designed by
Chapman Taylor in London, West One on Bond
Street tube station [8.21], and the London Pavilion
on Piccadilly Circus, the street entry led in to a
central space at what was revealed to be its
midpoint of vertical development. The fact that, in
the latter project, this occurred within the shell of
an existing building on the site, with a classical
tripartite subdivision of its elevations into *piano
rustica, piano nobile* and attic, which strongly
acknowledge street level as a base, only heightened
the sense of displacement within. Even more

135

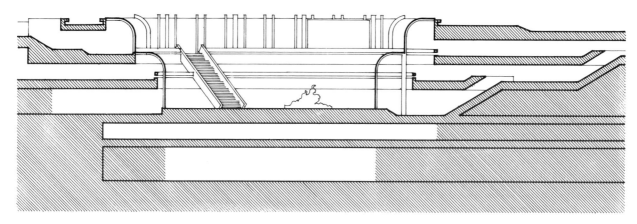

8.22 Forum des Halles, Paris: section through central
    space. 1 : 600.

8.23 Forum des Halles, Paris: view of central space.

dramatic in its subversion of the city datum, the
Forum des Halles in Paris was developed entirely
below ground level [8.22], from which it appeared
as a pit, with sides cascading down through open
courtyards of diminishing size [8.23]. The enclosed
mall networks, ringing these courts and extending
outwards from them [8.24], conversely grew in
extent the deeper they occurred and the closer they
approached the metro station, five levels below
ground.

In Montreal a whole series of such centres sprang
up along the invisible lines of the metro system,
and in particular around the stations of the
east–west route running through the upper city
centre, below the line of the Boulevard de
Maisonneuve. At McGill station, further north up
the Rue University from the Place Bonaventure
and Place Ville Marie developments in the lower
city centre, 2020 University was built in a form
similar to the London schemes, with a central
atrium well linking four retail levels, above and
below ground, with escalators, and with the
elevator banks of a twenty-two-storey central core
office building occupying one corner of the plan
[8.25]. In a neighbouring block, Les Terraces
elaborated the play of internal levels in a more

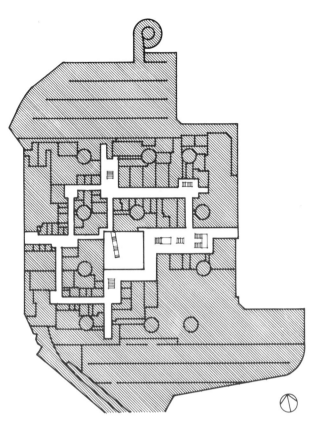

8.24 Forum des Halles, Paris: plan at lowest shopping mall level. 1 : 3,000.

8.25 2020 University, Montreal: view of central space.

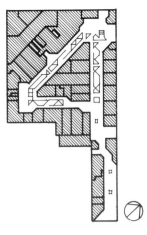

8.26 Les Terraces, Montreal: plan. 1 : 3,000.

complex way, by establishing a triangular mall arrangement in which the levels of the central block of shops were slipped in relation to those of the surrounding ring [8.26]. The mall was thus split along its lengths, with half-level flights of steps connecting mall seating areas on each side of the division and encouraging movement up and down the section [8.27]. To further complicate matters, the malls also changed levels from time to time down their length, so that, once entered from street or subway, the interior of the block appeared as a vertical maze, simple in plan but confusingly fragmented in section, in which it was impossible to establish an overall reference plane. Externally [8.28], the block envelope of the building, stepping back slightly as it rose from the pavement line, gave no indication of the complexity within.

Further to the east, along the same metro line, another Montreal city block was reconstructed at Les Galleries Dupuis [8.29], with two mall levels, street and subway, connected at a central escalator well and related to the Holiday Inn Hotel and an atrium office development occupying opposite corners of the block. Close by, and connected to the same metro station, Berri-de-Montigny, a more extensive development was undertaken for the University of Quebec in which a mall network in the lower levels, fronted by a mixture of commercial and student social uses, underpinned academic rather than commercial development above, but with a similar concentration on focal spaces formed at the centres of the two linked city blocks which made up the site, in one case with an atrium formed on the position of the nave of St Jacques' Church and incorporating fragments of the former building in the new structure.

At both Les Galleries Dupuis and the University of Quebec at Montreal, the sites incorporated several former block subdivisions within the new perimeter, and the same was true of another such development located midway between them and the McGill station in the city centre. In absorbing a number of former cross-streets, and replacing them

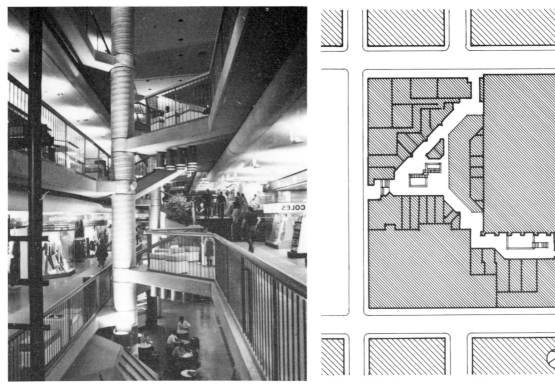

8.27 Les Terraces, Montreal: view of split-level malls.

8.29 Les Galleries Dupuis, Montreal: plan. 1 : 3,000.

8.28 Les Terraces, Montreal: view of exterior.

with the internal mall system, Le Complexe Desjardins thus similarly enlarged the bounding street grid, in this case to a 200-metre square dimension. In many ways the Desjardins project represents the simplest and clearest statement of the new pattern implicit in so many variations in the examples which have been mentioned. Within the new perimeter established for the development, four elevator cores, serving a hotel and three office towers above, were located in the four corner quadrants of the square plan [8.30]. Points of entry, either for pedestrians or, on the west side, for vehicles, occurred at the midpoints of the exterior sides, and at the centre of the plan a focal atrium space was formed [8.31], with escalator connections between main levels and overlooked by surrounding shopping galleries, hotel restaurants and office areas. Below street level a lower mall connected the atrium through to the Place des Arts cultural complex to the north, and to the adjoining metro station.

Through such projects then it is possible to trace the evolution in its most intensive form of the single cell which acts as the area-based, or 'parochial', component of the new pattern. Having established this characteristic form-type, the next step was to forge the system of horizontal connections which would transform it from a series of isolated, and somewhat anachronistic, units into a comprehensive pattern of development. Such connections, of a pragmatic kind, are evident in a number of the examples discussed. For example, 2020 University and Les Terraces are linked, not only to each other through their common connection to the subway, but also to the existing Eaton department store which occupies an adjacent site, thus forming an 'L' shaped group of subterraneously connected city blocks. Again, in the lower city centre of Montreal, Place Ville Marie was connected to Place Bonaventure through the intervening Central Station site, and on to the Place de la Victoria. In Toronto a similar series of expedient connections between adjoining developments was effected in the upper city centre along the north side of Bloor Street to form a string linking the Hudson's Bay Centre and the subway across Yonge Street to Two Bloor West, through the linear arcades of the Cumberland Terrace to Fifty Bloor West, and then across Bay Street to the Nu-West Centre.

The piecemeal formation of pedestrian linkages between shopping developments, often reinforced by circulation points for office towers, is a characteristic feature of many recent city centre developments, adapted in each case to the local urban pattern. In Sydney, for example, the attenuated north–south blocks of the commercial centre, between George, Pitt and Castlereagh Streets, encouraged the formation of numerous east–west Victorian arcades [8.32; 8.33], which provided cross-town pedestrian connections. The

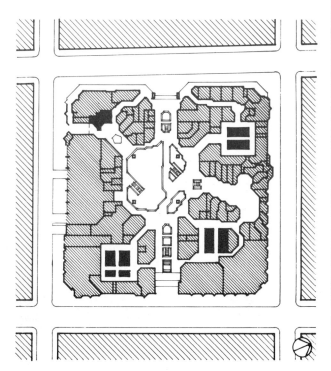

8.30 Le Complexe Desjardins, Montreal: plan at street level. 1 : 3,000.

8.31 Le Complexe Desjardins, Montreal: view of central atrium.

139

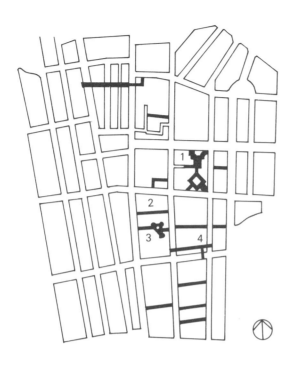

8.32 Sydney, Australia: plan of city centre with Victorian arcades and modern shopping malls forming cross-town connections through long city blocks. (1) MLC Centre; (2) Strand Arcade; (3) Mid City Centre; (4) Sydney Tower Centrepoint. 1 : 12,000.

8.34 MLC Centre, Sydney: view of 'Waterwall Fountain' sunken court serving shopping arcades below plaza. (Courtesy Harry Seidler and Associates)

8.33 Strand Arcade, Sydney: view of interior.

8.35 Mid City Centre, Sydney: view of arcade entrance to Pitt Street. (Courtesy Harry Seidler and associates)

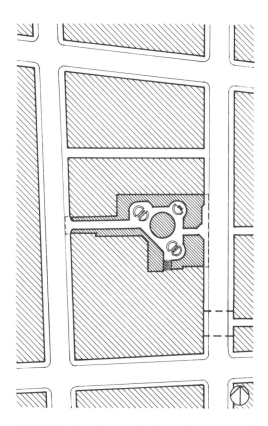

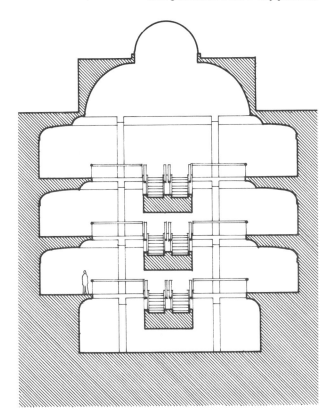

8.36 Mid City Centre, Sydney: plan at street level.
1 : 3,000.

8.37 Mid City Centre, Sydney: section through one of
three corner circulation spaces rising through the
shopping levels. 1 : 300.

modern arcades of the MLC Centre [8.34] and the
Mid City Centre [8.35], can be seen then as
continuations of that pattern, though in a more
intensive form, with, in the latter case, three full
trading levels and escalator and glass lift wells to
support them [8.36; 8.37]. The Mid City Centre,
however, also connects to Grace Brothers
department store alongside it, which in turn has a
two-storey bridge connection, containing restaurant
and display facilities [8.38], across Pitt Street to
malls below the Sydney Tower Centrepoint, which
again have a bridge link over Market Street to the
David Jones department store to the south.

If these examples indicate the strength of the
commercial impulse to bond individual components,
of separate ownership, into larger groups, despite
the inconvenience of vertical shifts of circulation
required to negotiate intervening streets, we may
look to a much earlier project to see this thrust
acknowledged in a co-ordinated plan. The site of
The Rockefeller Center development carried out in
the late 1930s occupied three Manhattan blocks,
each about 75 by 300 metres, between Fifth and
Sixth Avenues and 48th and 51st Streets. An
intermediate private cross-street, Rockefeller Plaza,
was introduced, to create six building plots which
were each developed to varying heights, but whose
cores were also linked by The Concourse, a system
of underground passages lined with shops and
exhibits and connecting to the subway. Thus,

although the design has been seen as distinctive in
respecting the street form of Manhattan at a time
when the Athens Charter was advocating the
destruction of the street,[2] it could also be seen as a
precursor of the Place Ville Marie form, in which
the podium roof is still tied to ground level, and
the towers still acknowledge plot boundaries. In
terms of our earlier analysis, the sunken Lower
Plaza, located at the centre of the development
[8.39], is significant, and in its equivocal
relationship to the two public circulation levels,
with their quite different characters, it may be
regarded either positively as 'a lush valley inside
the dry, flat New York grid . . . oasis-like' (Zeidler
1983:22), or negatively as 'turned into a skating
rink in '37 after a listless existence as shop window
entrance to the subterranean domain' (Koolhaas
1978:170). In either event, The Concourse at
Rockefeller Center introduced a new element in
the comprehensive planning of developments
covering more than one city block, and one which,
in terms of the displacement of pedestrian datum,
linkage of vertical circulation cores and creation of
a central focal space (albeit embryonic), anticipated
the post-war projects. And if these novel features
were there held in the background, as a pleasantly
unusual counterpoint to the dominant street grid
and plot-filling skyscraper format of Manhattan, we
might wonder what would happen if these
particular circumstances were removed.

141

8.38 Sydney, Australia: view of two-storey bridge link
across Pitt Street, connecting Grace Brothers
department store to the Sydney Tower Centrepoint.

8.39 Rockefeller Center, New York: view of Lower
Plaza.

8.40 Crystal City, Arlington, Virginia: view of entrance
pavilion to Crystal Underground Village.

One answer is illustrated by a project carried out
some fifty years later, and some 400 kilometres to
the south-west, in Arlington, Virginia. At first sight
the Crystal City development appears as a
conventional version of the Ville Radieuse
transformed into the post-war commercial precinct.
Isolated office and apartment towers clad in
concrete, aluminium and tinted glass are disposed
on the platform of an extensive plaza, gridded by
exposed aggregate paving strips and equipped with
concrete benches, planters, fountains and
monumental sculptures [8.40]. At lunch-time, on a
dull day, despite the large population which must
be housed inside the towers, the plaza is deserted.
However, in one corner stands a small pavilion
with the message 'Crystal Underground Village'
above the door. Stepping inside [8.41], we find
ourselves at the top of a double-height space, with
a stairway leading down to a small square filled
with people eating at tables or passing through to
the narrow streets which lead off in various
directions below the plaza. The crowded streets are
lined with shops of the Olde English
Emporium/Martha Washington Apple Pie variety
and connect the office cores [8.42]. They are
narrow, and entirely artificially lit, except at the
double-height entrance square, where a village
clock stands beside fast-food diners in a Wild West
Saloon. The materials used are brick, tile, plaster,
stone, timber and wrought iron.

In effect then, the development is two places
superimposed one upon the other [8.43]. One is the
Ville Radieuse reduced to its most peremptory
terms, the other Disneyland hyped to its most
agitated; one entirely open and public, but
deserted, the other hidden, private and crowded;
one all envelope, the other all frontage; one all
form, the other all content; one made in the
industrialised uniform of modern architecture, the
other in homespun kitsch. Entertaining as is the
schizophrenic journey between these two places, it
is difficult to resist the thought that they represent
Newcourt's ultimate revenge upon the city
conceived as a system of vehicular movement, as it
was developed from the Renaissance through the
Industrial Revolution and finally to the Ville
Radieuse. The Crystal City exists and is made
manifest, but in its final state of abstraction its
credibility depends upon its equally implausible
counter-form, the Underground Village, lurking in
the basement.

Yet, as a logical extension of the Rockefeller
Center format, removed from its Manhattan
context, Crystal City is immaculate. And as a
diagram of linkage, forming a convenient and
extensive pedestrian network between points of
vertical circulation, it offers some kind of precedent
for extending the system of parochial cells into a
full development pattern. But the network here
exists in isolation, underground, inducing no area-

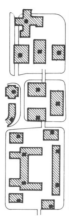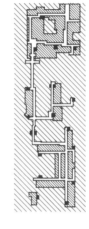

8.41 Crystal City, Arlington, Virginia: view inside entrance pavilion to Crystal Underground Village.

8.43 Crystal City, Arlington, Virginia: plans above ground (left) and below ground (Crystal Underground Village, right). 1 : 12,000.

8.42 Crystal City, Arlington, Virginia: view along mall in Crystal Underground Village.

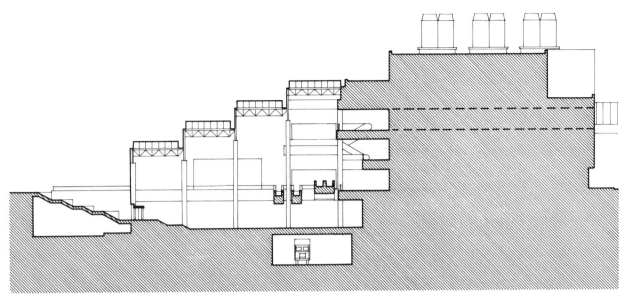

8.44 The Gallery at Market East, Philadelphia: section through atrium of The Gallery. 1 : 600.

8.45 The Gallery at Market East, Philadelphia: interior view of atrium in The Gallery.

based grouping or sectional rearrangement in the volumes above. For a more comprehensive reorganisation of development based on the idea of connections between adjoining city blocks, a series of other North American projects may be considered in which the retailing element acted as a more substantial binding force.

The first of these is the plan for the redevelopment of east Market Street in Philadelphia, traditionally the retail core of that city, but by the 1960s sharply in decline, with discount traders camping around the department stores which had remained. In 1960 the City Planning Commission adopted a plan proposed by Edmund Bacon for the renewal of the area, concentrating upon the reconstruction of five city blocks on the north side of Market Street, running east from City Hall. By 1977 the first phase of that plan, The Gallery at Market East, had been completed under an arrangement in which the city, acting as both ground landlord and construction manager, built the shell. This was then leased to the Rouse Company, who had provided one-third of the funding for the shell cost, the remainder being supplied by a grant from the Department of Housing and Urban Development (HUD). A major feature of The Gallery was an atrium, contained on three sides by the building and stepping down on the fourth towards an open (sunken) court and the street [8.44; 8.45]. Powerful as is the interior space created under the stepped glazed roof, the exterior, squeezed into a corner between a cross-street and the blank block of the new Gimbel's department store, relocated from across Market Street, appears modest and recessive [8.46]. The reason for this becomes apparent in the context of the full development plan, which establishes an axial pedestrian mall route down the centre of the five blocks, parallel to Market Street. The atrium of The Gallery – Gallery I in the sequence of the full development – is thus not a major focus of the street, but is instead performing the difficult

8.46 The Gallery at Market East, Philadelphia: exterior
view of main entrance from Market Street.

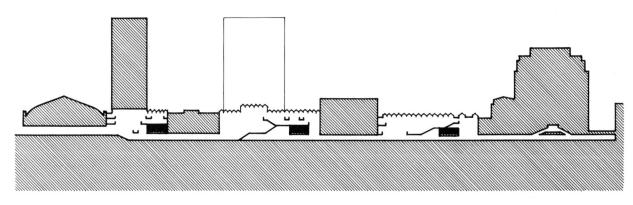

8.47 Market Street East Development, Philadelphia:
section through eventual extent of redevelopment of
north side of Market Street East, with phase one,
The Gallery, as the most easterly (right) of a
sequence of linked atria formed within the city
blocks. Cross-streets (9th to 11th) passing through
the development are shown solid black. 1 : 3,000.

architectural task of breaking into the side of a
strong linear spine route from a street whose
frontages are now turned inward. It is proposed to
straddle the central route with a series of office
blocks and department stores, of which Gimbels
and the existing Strawbridge and Clothier define
the first phase, and these subdivide the route into
component atria (Galleries I, II and III) linked by
malls which dive under the obstructions and
connect to the subway stations below [8.47]. The
long section through the completed development
thus proposes a sequence of voids and solids, atria

and department stores (which themselves may
contain smaller atria, as in the proposal for J. C.
Penney, the next store in the sequence) which are
welded together in a continuous structure through
which the existing cross-streets, 9th to 11th,
penetrate as tubes.

Market Street East may then be seen as
achieving the same end of lateral pedestrian
connections between city blocks as did Crystal City,
but in a way which engaged the whole section of
the building and influenced the development form
at all levels. An even more complete fusion of plan

and section occurred in the Toronto Eaton Centre, which followed the same principle of establishing a new axial route down the centre of blocks fronting a major existing shopping street, Yonge Street. In this case the former pattern of blocks and streets did not impose a subdivision of the new development, which absorbed some 400 metres of previously interrupted frontage along the west side of Yonge Street to form a continuous development between Queen Street and Dundas Street. Nevertheless, and despite the powerful continuity of the internal vaulted mall, previously described, which in effect unites two-thirds of this length in a single linear atrium, a notional articulation of the building around four node foci was established by the architects [8.48]. At these points the shop frontages were held back to broaden the circulation

8.48 Eaton Centre, Toronto: node structure diagram (after sketch diagrams prepared by the architects). 1 : 12,000.

space, at the base of the atrium section escalators were inserted to connect mall levels, and side malls led out of the centre, to east and west in the two middle node positions and by bridge to Simpson's department store on the other side of Queen Street in the case of the southern one, which also connected with the subway station at basement level.

A more consistently determined attempt was made at the Eaton Centre to create frontage to the main street alongside which it runs than was the case at Market Street East or at the other downtown shopping centres, such as Plaza Pasadena and Buffalo Main Place, which were discussed in Chapter 6. Shallow, outward-facing shop units were located along the street, and the elevation was treated as a lightweight metal screen, detached from the building behind and provided with a variety of architectural incident [8.49]. Nevertheless there can be no disguising the fact that this is a subsidiary feature in the overall hierarchy of events, and that the main action occurs in a parallel zone behind, hidden from the street and approached, not frontally as in the Milan Galleria, but, as at Market Street East, from the

8.49 Eaton Centre, Toronto: view of east elevation to Yonge Street.

8.50 Eaton Centre, Toronto: view of northern entrance at corner of Yonge Street and Dundas Street.

8.51 Eaton Centre, Toronto: interior view of northern entrance.

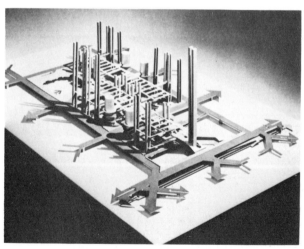

8.52 Yerba Buena Project, San Francisco: model of circulation systems.

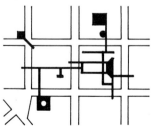

8.53 Peachtree Center, Atlanta, Georgia: network of cross-block pedestrian circulation. 1 : 12,000.

flank. Where an apparently frontal portal does occur, at the northern node space on the corner of Yonge and Dundas [8.50], it is connected to the main mall only indirectly, through the intervening Eaton department store [8.51]. Despite the conciliatory gestures to the street then, the centre unmistakably belongs to the new pattern, developed here to the point where its internal connections have expanded to form a single unified volume which dominates the section. In terms of the evolution of that pattern, the Eaton Centre and Crystal City thus represent two extreme solutions to the question of how a system of connections might be arranged to weld the individual pedestrian cells into an extensive urban structure.

Three further North American projects may serve to illustrate the variety of building solutions which could be developed within these options. In 1969 Kenzo Tange prepared a plan for an extended mixed-use project in an area south of Market Street in central San Francisco, as the nucleus of the Yerba Buena Center Redevelopment Plan, then mooted. The scheme simplified the existing city street pattern into three blocks running south from Market Street between 3rd and 4th Streets, and was intended to comprise a variety of commercial, leisure, cultural and car parking elements. The framework for the planning of these was conceived in an almost literal sense as the pedestrian circulation system, demonstrated in a development model in which it stands as a skeleton awaiting the attachment of surrounding user volumes [8.52].

Two features, familiar from the preceding discussion, distinguished this system, the first being the network character of routes, which connected across the blocks and included a moving pavement down the length of the development, and the second being central focal spaces in each block. The latter were described as 'Galleria', a term which had achieved sufficient currency by that date to convey the cohesive, but functionally non-specific role they played. As the architects noted, 'When we met the men responsible for constructing and operating individual buildings, architects and others, the word Galleria had found its way into their thinking and provided a means for reaching a consensus.' Around these Galleria and the linking pedestrian route network, the various uses were arranged according to their need for access to the prime pedestrian areas in the centre of the blocks (shopping, hotel, restaurant and banqueting spaces, cultural uses) or vehicular access from the edges (car parks, office buildings).

A similar mixture of uses is present in the Peachtree Center complex developed by John Portman in Atlanta, where some seven blocks of the city centre have been linked and, to a greater or lesser degree, redeveloped [8.53]. Ducking and weaving around remaining existing buildings in the blocks, the development forms a more contingent assembly than Tange's comprehensive plan, and is punctuated by two of the hotel atria for which Portman is famous, the Peachtree Plaza and the Hyatt Regency. A little further down San

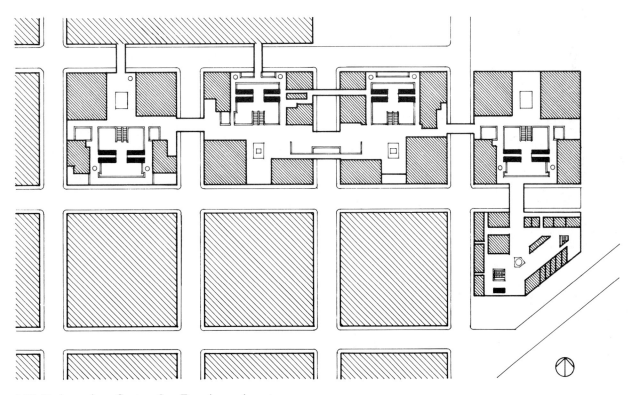

8.54 Embarcadero Center, San Francisco: plan at upper mall level. 1 : 3,000.

8.55 Embarcadero Center, San Francisco: view of central
court in one of the four shopping blocks.

8.56 Embarcadero Center, San Francisco: view of atrium
of Hyatt Regency Hotel, forming termination of
sequence of linked shopping blocks.

Francisco's Market Street from the Yerba Buena site, Portman has built another centre, the Embarcadero, in which the simple diagram implicit in these developments could be more clearly applied [8.54]. A line of four smaller city blocks was developed as a string of almost identical components, with cruciform mall plans extending out from central escalator courts [8.55], to bridge east–west to adjoining blocks in the sequence, and, in the case of the more westerly pair, northwards as well, to the neighbouring Golden Gateway Center. Each block formed a three-storey shopping podium to an office slab above, whose core was displaced from the central east–west axis, at the eastern end of which a fifth block terminated the sequence in the spectacular central atrium of the Hyatt Regency San Francisco [8.56].

Taken together with the larger European central area shopping projects discussed earlier, these North American examples thus amount to a considerable body of work in which the principles of the inverted pattern of development, both in individual 'cells' and in more extended networks, may be seen to apply. A final question which might then be asked concerns the extent to which such a principle might be applied. If two or three city blocks may be reorganised in this way, why not twenty or thirty? Or is there some physical limitation beyond which further growth becomes impractical, as seemed to be the case with the out-of-town shopping centres at about six primary and intermediate nodes?

Certainly in terms of individual central area developments, such as Eldon Square and the Manchester Arndale in England, or the Eaton Centre in Canada, a similar order of magnitude applies, but this is perhaps more to do with the limits of land acquisition and financial resources of any single developer than with an inherent ceiling beyond which the principle becomes inoperative. For in a number of cities a combination of private advantage and public aspiration has acted to extend it far beyond the scope of the individual developer and has created networks which embrace the whole central area and begin to rival and displace the former street network through which they penetrate. In two of the cities referred to in connection with individual developments, Toronto and Montreal, the genesis of such a comprehensive pedestrian route system is apparent. In Toronto, apart from the series of connections which run along Bloor Street in the upper city centre, a system of underground walkways in the lower business area extends from the Eaton Centre down through the Toronto-Dominion Centre to Union Station, about 800 metres to the south. At Montreal a more elaborate set of possibilities was opened up by the migration of the central business district (CBD) northwards from the harbour area into the central ground between upper and lower parts of the city during the 1960s. This took the form of a series of major developments on large

sites held by the Canadian National (CN) and Canadian Pacific railroads, beginning with Place Ville Marie. Making use of the basement space already created by the former tracks and marshalling yards, these developments began, as we have seen, to form underground interconnections between lower retail floors. By 1966 this feature was sufficiently marked for Vincent Ponte, who had been retained as a consultant planner for the CN site, to visualise it as a comprehensive and revolutionary device for restructuring the city core: 'Planners are beginning to go beyond the 2-D of paper plans. In this city we are concentrating the core functions into a tight totally interrelated unit, doubling and tripling the use of the same parcels of precious Downtown land by inserting several levels above and below ground.'[3]

In the following year Ponte prepared a plan illustrating the extension of the system across the whole core area, and linking about half of the blocks within a rectangle about 700 × 1,000 metres defined by the metro stations of Bonaventure, Victoria, McGill and Peel [8.57]. Subsequent developments, such as 2020 University and Les Terraces, have filled in further sections of this plan, which envisaged some 10 kilometres of covered pedestrian routes, and in addition, as was described earlier in this chapter, the system has pupped a series of satellite growths around the Place des Arts and Berri-de-Montigny metro stations to the east.

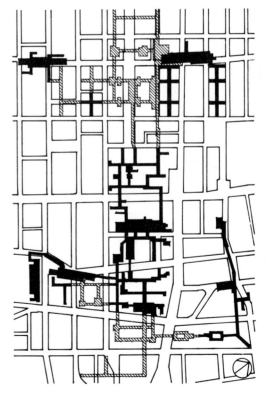

8.57 Montreal: plan of existing (black) and proposed (hatched) enclosed pedestrian routes described by Vincent Ponte in 1966.

151

8.58 Queen's Arcade, Leeds.

In Europe a number of cities toyed with plans for a similar reconstruction of the pedestrian circulation in the central area at this time. On a similarly sloping site to Montreal's, the English city of Leeds prepared an ambitious plan in which the main east–west shopping street, Commercial Street, would be pedestrianised as the datum axis of a grade-separated pedestrian network which would run overhead on the lower ground to the south and underground on the upper slope to the north. Although a number of new building owners in the lower city were persuaded to incorporate upper-level walkways in their construction, these now stand as isolated and anachronistic features, and instead a more limited ground-level network has been achieved, linking the city's Victorian arcades [8.58], by way of pedestrianised streets [8.59], and recent covered shopping malls. This approach, of creating a gradually expanded pedestrianised street system, has obvious economical and conservationist advantages and has been generally adopted in European cities, although it should be noted that it contains several topographical features of the new pattern, such as the broadening of the traffic street network as streets are closed off, and the effective introversion of blocks of development in relation to that network. The fact that the 'introverted' frontages are the same street fronts as before,

8.59 Leeds: pedestrianisation in central area connecting earlier arcade routes.

rather than enclosed malls and atria, disguises this fact which is nevertheless apparent to the motorist who now skirts around their perimeter, vainly trying to identify where the city centre actually is.

The notion of fully grade-separated pedestrian networks was not a new one of course, and was discussed by Le Corbusier in 'Towards a New Architecture', in which he castigated Auguste Perret for being 'so far carried away' as to throw 'a veil of dangerous futurism over what was a sound idea' (the City of Towers) by suggesting a system of pedestrian bridges linking the towers; '. . . for what purpose? . . . the inhabitants . . . would never have the slightest desire to take their exercise on giddy bridges' (Le Corbusier 1927:56). And while it was an idea which proved difficult to apply on a comprehensive scale to the central areas of existing European cities, it was carried out on several green-field projects, and notably in the town centre of Runcorn New Town in England, in which an extended upper-level pedestrian network was formed across both the malls of the shopping centre, and the access decks of Stirling and Wilford's adjacent Southgate housing area [8.60].

In terms of the development of fully articulated pedestrian networks within existing city centres however, the most comprehensive implementation has occurred in North America, and notably in six

cities – Minneapolis, St Paul, Spokane, Cincinnati, Houston and Calgary – in which the system has been executed to a remarkable degree. Although the stated general objectives of these projects – to ease congestion and traffic conflict at street level and provide a comfortable pedestrian environment in adverse weather – were common to them all, the initiatives for their inception and the methods of their funding and subsequent extension were so varied that they cannot be categorised simply as the products of excessively ambitious city authorities. Indeed the longest established of them, at Houston, which was begun as early as 1947, has been entirely developed by individual owners making cut-and-cover tunnel connections between blocks, and remains a system of completely private underground routes extending now some 4.5 kilometres in length, linking fifty buildings, and accessible to the general public through their entrance lobbies [8.61].

The Houston preference for tunnel links was not followed in the other five cities, which opted for upper-level systems, with bridges. Nevertheless, the earliest examples of these, which occurred in the early 1960s in Spokane and Minneapolis, were again carried out by private developers acting independently to form connections to existing department stores and hence to create spontaneous

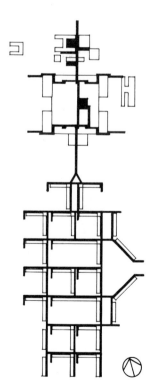

8.60 Runcorn New Town, England: network of grade-separated pedestrian routes as constructed to date, linking the malls of Shopping City in the north, to the access decks of Southgate housing in the south. 1 : 12,000.

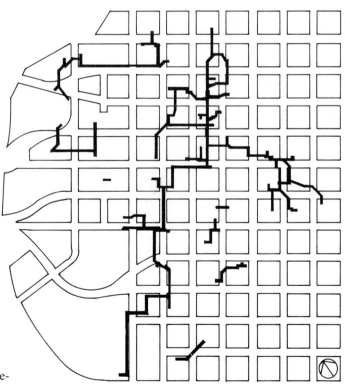

8.61 Houston, Texas: plan of underground tunnels forming cross-block pedestrian connections, at 1982. 1 : 12,000.

8.62 Spokane, Washington: view of three Skywalk bridges
crossing Howard Street in the central area. (Courtesy
Lyle Balderson)

8.63 Cincinnati, Ohio: open precinct at high level on the
Skywalk system in the central area.

shopping mall arrangements in the city centre analogous to, and competitive with, those being developed out of town [8.62]. In this way networks began to be developed in those two cities, almost entirely funded and managed by the private sector, and which attracted the attention of public planning agencies elsewhere. The most ambitious piece of public funding then occurred in St Paul, where a demonstration project was supported by a large grant from HUD, used to purchase public easement rights through buildings and construct almost thirty connecting bridges. Private developers were then encouraged to extend this system by constructing further bridges at their own cost.

At Cincinnati the costs of constructing the Skywalk [8.63], were met by the city, which spent $5.8 million between 1969 and 1973 in implementing the first phase of covered walkways, from the Convention Center to Fountain Square, the principal public square in the city, and built over an alley between existing buildings. Between 1976 and 1979 a further $2 million was spent expanding this route with totally enclosed, heated and air-conditioned walkways connecting major department stores in the central area [8.64]. An important feature of the Cincinnati Skywalk, as of the St Paul scheme, was its character as a comprehensively planned network, rather than as a fortuitous collection of bridge links. As parts of the central area came up for redevelopment, owners were required to accommodate the anticipated extensions of the system, providing frontage at the upper level and taking on the maintenance and running costs of the connecting bridges which were paid for by the city.

The differing perceptions of public and private benefit to be gained from these systems are considerable. In contrast to Minneapolis and Spokane, private developers in Cincinnati were initially unenthusiastic about the project. Rather it was the city authorities who had, for many years, been concerned with the inadequacy of the pedestrian system at ground level. As early as 1925 the *Official Plan of the City of Cincinnati* had discussed the problem of enlarging carriageway widths at the expense of sidewalks to take increased vehicular traffic, and had debated the possibility of both overhead and underground sidewalks to supplement pedestrian routes, but had concluded that the practical difficulties were such that, 'at even a very small cost, [they] would be inadvisable'.[4] With the completion of some sixteen bridge connections in the core, however, and plans for extensive expansion of the system beyond, businesses now regard it as a benefit and promote its activities in a weekly newspaper *The Skywalk News*.

Perhaps the most remarkable of all these experiments, in terms of both the extent and method of implementation, is the Plus 15 system at Calgary, Alberta, where by 1982 thirty bridges had been constructed and a further twenty-two

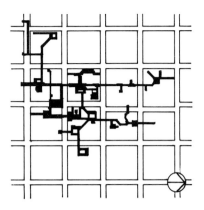

8.64 Cincinnati, Ohio: plan of extent of Skywalk system in the central area at December 1977. 1 : 12,000.

approved in accordance with a plan prepared by the City Planning Department, but financed by individual developers [8.65]. This was achieved by means of an elaborate development control system of 'bonuses', by which developers were led to construct portions of the pedestrian network (nominally '+15' feet above grade) in exchange for development density gains. The code governing this system read like the gaming rules of some ingenious variant of Monopoly, according to which developers could progressively improve upon the notional plot ratio of 8.0 FAR (floor to site area ratio) in the city centre by the incorporation of individual features of the Plus 15 network, each of which yielded a specific bonus. The most enticing bonus, with 30 sq. metres of development area gained for each 1 sq. metre of Plus 15 system created, applied to the creation of bridge links, but in order to reach this bonus the developer had to work his way through lower-bonus features, such as open space at grade and +15 levels. In this way adept players of the game might boost plot densities as high as 20 FAR, while the city would gain another section of its planned network, at no cost to itself.

The origins of this intriguing system lay in proposals made in the late 1960s for the urban renewal of Calgary, by the firm of Affleck, Desbarats, Dimakapoulos, Lebensold and Sise, who had been architects for the Place Bonaventure project in Montreal. These were taken up by Harold Hanen and David Diver in the City Planning Department under the direction of M. H. Rogers and developed into the 1970 Calgary Plan, followed by Development Control By-law No. 8,600 which laid down the rules of the bonus system. This was accompanied by a tripartite zoning of the city centre within which variants of the rules would apply in differing degrees of intensity, from area A in the CBD, where developments must have at least half of the ground-floor area and +15 frontage devoted to retail, cultural, entertainment, service or amusement facilities, to the residential area C.

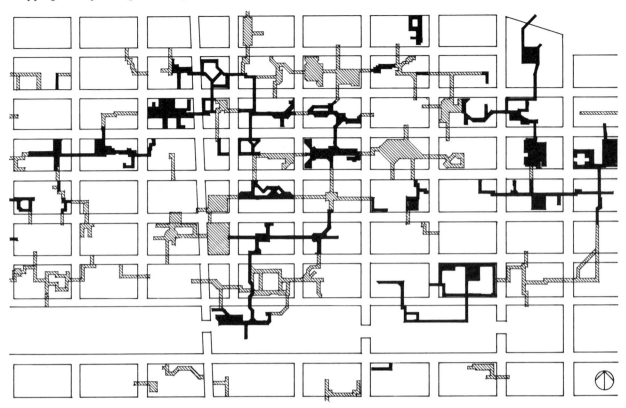

8.65 Calgary: plan of central area showing extent of
existing (black) and approved or proposed (hatched)
routes on the Plus 15 Skyway system in 1982.
1 : 12,000.

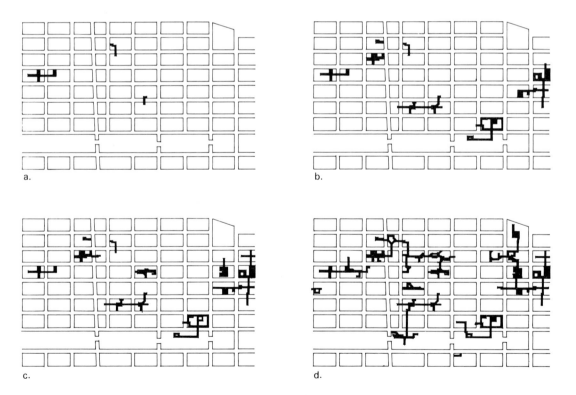

8.66 Calgary: plans showing growth of Plus 15 system in
the central area, showing extent of development: (a)
from 1970 to 1972; (b) by 1975; (c) by 1978; (d) by
1982.

8.67 Calgary: double-deck bridge at +15 and +30 across 7th Avenue into the Nova Building. (Courtesy John Abel)

Initially directed primarily to air-rights development of public open space over back lanes within city blocks, the system ran into technical difficulties with building codes concerned with means of escape and with the excessive height requirement (6.7 metres) of garbage tip trucks, and gradually shifted emphasis to the provision of fully air-conditioned routes connecting city blocks. As the system grew [8.66], in some areas developing +30 bridges on top of the +15 [8.67], the city was encouraged to move to a mandatory implementation, and in 1976 adopted the 'Plus 15 Must Policy' by which minimum requirements of the system were to be implemented regardless of bonus utilisation. Where developers took up bonus options beyond the mandatory limit, they were allowed to give benefits to the city in cash rather than kind, and a +15 Cash-in-lieu Fund was established with which priority sections of the system elsewhere could be implemented directly by the city authorities.

If the histories of public and private initiative in generating the grade-separated pedestrian systems in these six cities could hardly be more varied, the outcome has been increasingly to encourage a view of the city centre as a single managed enterprise. In each case the city authorities regard their experiment as a success, although the investment they have entailed no doubt generates its own commitment. Technical problems relating to means

of escape, clearance and environmental control have been largely overcome, although in Cincinnati the differences between air-conditioning systems used in individual buildings, some positively pressurised and some negatively, has resulted in a greater compartmentation of the Skywalk than was intended. All six cities have developed more or less extensive design guidelines for visible components of the system, such as the structure, cladding, internal and external lighting and internal finishes of bridges for example, and have recognised the importance of integrated signage in navigating the routes [8.68], and of adequate provision of elevator connections between levels for the handicapped. In a few cases, such as Cincinnati and Calgary, the system is designed to be open for twenty-four hours, and the Cincinnati police have found the Skywalk to be safer and less prone to vandalism than the streets outside, although the high cost of foot patrols has led to proposals in Calgary for the selective closure of less intensively used sections at night, and for a greater degree of closed-circuit television (CCTV) surveillance.

However, the most problematic issue with all of these systems concerns their relationship to the existing network of the street, and the degree to which they complement or threaten each other. While under development, each unit of frontage and activity added to the new system could be regarded as an achievement and a positive gain.

8.68 Cincinnati, Ohio: information panel in the Skywalk.

But once the new system became established, the corollary, that each gain to the pedestrian network was a loss to the street, became more apparent. The degree and significance of this shift is generally difficult to determine, but a walk on a hot and sticky afternoon through downtown Houston suggests that considerable areas of the city streets have been largely abandoned by pedestrians for the air-conditioned comfort below [8.69]. In Calgary some objective assessment has been possible in the core retailing area, between the Bay and Eaton's department stores, where pedestrian levels at +15 and +30 coexist with a pedestrianised main street, 8th Avenue [8.70]. During fine weather at least, the latter remains the most densely used pedestrian route in the city, yet in terms of retail trade, the upper levels are most successful, with grade ranking third.[5] In order to retain activity on the street frontage, if not at street level, Calgary experimented with running the +15 routes around the perimeter of blocks, but abandoned this in favour of central routes, so that the rule for area 'C' residential development, for example, now reads 'All development must provide for or allow for future development of +15 public pedestrian easements at the mid-points of the block North–South and East–West, and be a minimum of 6.1 metres wide.'[6]

8.69 Houston, Texas: Louisiana Street; the pedestrians are nearly all underground or, in this case, in one of the few overhead connections between city blocks.

Other cities have similarly experienced the commercial pressures by which the pedestrian system, once established, is encouraged to grow. In the centre of Spokane rental levels for retail space on the upper level now equal or exceed those at street level. Similarly in Minneapolis, income from buildings on the skyway is estimated to be 10 per cent higher than that from similar buildings not so connected (Irvin and Groy 1982:7).

Whether or not the economic and environmental attractions of the segregated networks will seriously damage ground-level frontage on a broad scale, concern has been expressed over the visual intrusion of the upper-level systems upon the street, and particularly in Calgary where street-level views of the dramatic escarpment formed by the curve of the Bow River in which the city centre lies, have been blocked by +15 bridges.

It may be said that these reservations are inevitable features of the ambitious skywalk approach, but it might also be argued that they have weight because, paradoxically, the systems adopted in these North American cities have not been ambitious enough. Conceived and

implemented essentially as systems of *circulation* they have failed to develop corresponding patterns of *organisation*, which would transform them into complete and satisfying urban structures. In terms of our earlier analysis, we could say that they have successfully achieved an integrated pedestrian network, with all the uncomfortable effects of frontage inversion and datum displacement which this implies for the external street system, but have not yet developed a corresponding Newcourt-like parochial organisational pattern, which would bring the compensating advantages of spatial identity and functional integration within the new system. Thus the skywalk routes in the various cities have almost entirely failed to develop node spaces which would provide a sense of place and hierarchy in the system. There are exceptions to this, and notably in Minneapolis where a number of atria such as the IDS Crystal Court articulate the network. Again the Calgary planning rules encourage the creation of larger public spaces, such as the enclosed park, the Devonshire Gardens, which has been formed at +45 level of Toronto Dominion Square [8.71], while the Cincinnati planners have shifted emphasis

8.70 Calgary: view of pedestrianised 8th Avenue beside Toronto Dominion Square (right) looking west. Plans to cover this street as part of the redevelopment of the block on the south side (left) have been prepared. (Courtesy John Abel)

8.71 Calgary: the Devonian Gardens on the fourth level of Toronto Dominion Square. (Courtesy John Abel)

159

8.72 Pulteney Bridge, Bath: view along street crossing the bridge, with shops on each side.

8.73 Pulteney Bridge, Bath: view of 'outside' of bridge.

on vertical circulation points from the street bridges to internal atria within the blocks. However, the overriding impression of the greater part of these systems is of an unstructured network of corridors, environmentally comfortable, but devoid of the vitality of the street. This is exacerbated by the fact that, since the routes are to be considered as essentially the solution to a circulation problem, rather than as the zones of primary activity in an area-based reorganisation of urban functions, the linking bridges are regarded, in the emasculated terms of development control, as 'foils' and 'neutral architectural elements' in which no other activity but circulation may occur. They therefore remain empty corridors rather than streets, with all that that term implies, and in the sense that the Ponte Vecchio in Florence, the Ponte di Rialto in Venice and the Pulteney Bridge in Bath [*8.72*; *8.73*], or indeed the cross-street connections of the Gallery at Market East in Philadelphia, function as streets.

The city skywalk systems may perhaps thus be properly regarded, not as comprehensive extensions of the patterns of organisation which we have seen to develop in downtown malls, but rather as abstractions of one single aspect of those patterns, concerned with linkage and segregated pedestrian circulation. In this they can be seen as a further development of the programme for the rationalisation of the city's systems, in which a new layer, the pedestrian grid, has been isolated and superimposed upon the earlier grid abstractions of traffic and land-use. And if this distinction may seem a fine one, it may be worth concluding with a consideration of some precedents for this in modern planning theory, and also of the way in which this solution would differ from a true area-based structure for the city.

Notes

1. See article by Saxon, R. G., 'The great indoors', *Architectural Review*, vol. 165, no. 985, Mar. 1979: 161–3; and Saxon, R. G. 1983.

2. By Zeidler, (1983:22), for example. Zeidler suggests that, in contrast to the CIAM proposals, Rockefeller Center 'pointed in another, older direction, one re-scaled to the modern city'. In this, however, he refers to its respect of plot lines and incorporation of varied uses, rather than to its underground pedestrian network.

3. *Architectural Forum*, Sept. 1966.

4. City of Cincinnati, City Planning Commission, *Official Plan of the City of Cincinnati: 1925*. Cincinnati, 1925:98. Quoted by Forusz, 1981:335.

5. Cited by Collins, D., Sinclair, D. and Tennent, C. in *The Plus 15 in Downtown Calgary: An Innovative Grade Separated Pedestrian Movement System*, paper given at Plus 15 Seminar in Calgary, 30 Apr. 1982.

6. City of Calgary, *Development Control By-law No. 8,600*, Section 42(10), para (e).

Chapter 9 Conclusion: towards an integrated structure

By the late 1970s there was a general feeling among North American developers and architects that a major period of shopping centre expansion had passed. Opportunities still existed for large schemes, particularly overseas, but a combination of expensive money, reduced demand and saturation of many areas of the domestic market with new centres caused people to speak wistfully of the great days of the 1960s and the impossibility of repeating the billion dollar scale of such projects as the Toronto Eaton Centre. This perception was reinforced by other factors, and notably the demise of US central government funding through HUD, which had been instrumental in getting many of the most adventurous schemes, from Faneuil Hall and Market Street East to the St Paul Skywalk system, off the ground. It was also confirmed by statistics, for between 1976 and 1979 the proportion of centres under way in the US with a GLA in excess of 60,000 sq. metres declined from 7.3 per cent of the market to only 2.7 per cent, while the proportion of small developments, with a GLA below 10,000 sq. metres, rose to almost 60 per cent.[1] Thus observers could suggest that 'the super regional center will go the way of the dinosaur' (Gruen 1978:9), and design attention shifted to energy-saving measures, adapting to smaller cars, and the refurbishment of earlier centres which were now looking the worse for wear.

In the UK a similar shift of mood occurred. After the shock of the 1973 recession and accompanying collapse of the property market, many of the largest developers, who had begun with a few hundred pounds capital soon after the Second World War and expanded into multi-million pound corporations during the years of growth,[2] withdrew altogether from new projects. Their place was taken by new companies which concentrated upon the previously neglected second-tier scale of district centres, as at Hempstead Valley in Kent [9.1], or out-of-town superstores and hypermarkets.

9.1 Hempstead Valley Centre, Gillingham, England: view of roof structure at junction in malls.

In retrospect then, the period from about 1950 to 1975 seemed to represent a complete cycle of development. During this time the shopping mall, beginning as an inconsequential space between free-standing stores, had passed through its phases of invention, with its enclosure in the 1950s, of rapid growth and prolific reproduction during the 1960s, and of culmination in a series of major projects during the 1970s. Against this background other themes had become apparent, and particularly in its closing stages. High energy costs symptomatic of the final stage of the cycle caused a re-examination of the totally artificial environment which had been the predominant tendency of mall design, and prompted a return to earlier models of space enclosure. Specialty centres, themselves a product of the unprecedented prosperity of the latter years of the upwave, nevertheless posed fundamental criticisms of the whole outcome of the development of the shopping mall, of what was seen as its bland, repetitive styles of trading and architecture, of its indifference to locality and of its destruction of traditional urban patterns.

Seen in this light, the evolution of the modern shopping mall may appear as only the most recent of a succession of similar waves of this type of development which have accompanied periods of economic growth in the past. In the prosperity of the early years of the nineteenth century some of the first such experiments occurred, as in the Royal Opera Arcade (1816) and Burlington Arcade (1818) in London. During the boom period of the middle decades of the century a whole crop of major arcades appeared across Europe, including Sillem's Bazaar in Hamburg (1845), the Galeries St Hubert in Brussels (1847), the Galleria Vittorio Emanuele II in Milan (1867) and the Barton Arcade in Manchester (1871). Finally, the period of economic growth preceding the First World War produced the Cleveland Arcade in Cleveland, Ohio (1890), the New Trade Halls (GUM) in Moscow (1893), the Galleria Umberto I in Naples (1891) and Friedrichstrassenpassage in Berlin (1908).

These earlier periods of experiment in the enclosure of public space associated with shopping bear comparison with that of the recent past, both in their novelty and in terms of the scale of the most ambitious projects (the mall cross-section of the Galleria Umberto I is almost identical to that of the Eaton Centre). But if we might then argue that the post-war development of the shopping mall represents a chapter in a continuing progress, and one which is now effectively completed, it should also be said that individual projects do not fall neatly into restricted periods of long-term economic cycles, and new solutions will continue to emerge. Major programmes are still being planned, and some of them very large indeed. The Rouse Company is engaged in the South Street Seaport development in Manhattan, while Cadillac Fairview, the developers of the Eaton Centre and the White Plains Galleria, is undertaking the enormous Houston Center project, extending over thirty blocks of downtown Houston and said to cost in excess of $5 billion. In addition, recessions often stimulate innovation, a classic example being that of the supermarket, which first appeared as a cost-cutting response to the Depression of the 1930s. In this respect, the new emphasis upon the renovation and closure of first-generation centre malls has encouraged the use of lightweight fabric structures, whose translucency solves the problems of mall enclosure and natural lighting in a novel way.

One of the first such applications of modern coated fabrics was at the Marl Shopping Centre in Marl, West Germany, in which a double-skin, pressurised fabric roof was used to cover a rectangular two-storey mall space in three abutting sections, each 53.8 metres long and 29 metres wide. A few years later, in 1978, the upper floor of the Bullocks department store in the Oakridge Mall in San Jose, California, was enclosed with a 1,700-sq. metre tent-like fabric roof, supported on light arched ribs, and with a non-structural second fabric layer internally at the insistence of fire code officials, and providing a degree of additional thermal insulation. The outer skin of this roof was formed in a Teflon-coated fibreglass fabric, which was used again for the Florida Festival, a shopping

9.2 Basildon Town Square, England: model of proposal for the refurbishment of an early New Town precinct, using a fabric roof structure. (Courtesy Michael Hopkins Architects)

and entertainment centre at Sea World in Orlando, and in 1982 the same material was used in its first application to a refurbished mall, in a tensioned fabric covering to the Mall at 163rd Street in Miami.

In the UK, Michael Hopkins Architects' and Buro Happold's project for the enclosure of the Town Square in Basildon [9.2], one of the earliest New Towns, has demonstrated the elegant possibilities for inserting mast-suspended lightweight fabric structures into existing locations which may require modernisation, in Basildon's case because of the construction of a new enclosed mall, the Phase 2 Eastgate Centre, near by. In a similar proposal for Sunderland, Building Design Partnership demonstrated the full range of upgrading options which could apply from relandscaping the open street, through lightweight enclosure, to full environmental control with insulated roof structure, and illustrated the interdependence of building control, funding and centre management issues which can apply to such projects. Often initiated less by the prospect of an immediate rental return on the capital cost as by the fear of a drastic decline in an existing investment threatened by more modern competing facilities, they have resulted in complex and

extensive remodelling exercises, usually undertaken while trading continues in the existing shops. In the Sharpstown Center in Houston, for example, built in 1960, some 100 stores were added in 1976 and a further 89 in 1980 on a new second level constructed on top of the existing buildings. Again, at Lennox Square Mall in Atlanta, the Plaza Court project entailed the expansion and renovation of 9,290 sq. metres of retail space on three levels around an atrium formed by the enclosure of 2,600 sq. metres of an open plaza.

As a building- or form-type then, the mall will undergo further development, albeit on a more modest scale than in the immediate past, and in ways which may be expected to acknowledge the critique which the specialty centre variants have suggested of the classic models of the 1960s and early 1970s. Those models stand as a diverse body of experiments in the enclosure of public space, sometimes internalising it in monumental versions of the private grotto, sometimes extending the technical possibilities of the nineteenth-century arcade, and always pursuing the notion of the pedestrian street as a carefully contrived and highly seductive passage of exchange.

But if the mall as form-type can be conveniently summarised in this way, and regarded as a building solution which will continue to develop in certain directions, its implications for the city around it, with which the second part of this book has been concerned, are not so readily concluded. The great numbers of developments which have been undertaken since the Second World War, and the radical novelty of their patterns of location and organisation, constitute a challenge to traditional forms of urban development which, it is contended here, can hardly be regarded as a temporary aberration from which recession, and a more widespread public support for conservationist and conservative planning policies, have now saved us. For running through all those developments is a thread of assumptions about the nature of public space, the way it is organised and controlled, and the way it relates to the city outside, which leaves a great unanswered question for the future. This is not a question about the economic effects of the new centres upon cities, for while some have undoubtedly exacerbated the impoverishment of historic centres, others have stimulated the regeneration of areas, such as Yonge Street in Toronto or the Inner Harbor in Baltimore, which were in decline. Nor is it solely a question of the social impact of redevelopment, which drives out small, established traders, and disrupts existing communities, for in this respect the new centres are the symptoms, rather than the causes, of change. Nor indeed is it a matter of the appearance of buildings, for, as we have seen, architectural manners can be modified to acknowledge their context. Rather, it is a question primarily about the form and structure of urban development, and it is one which, even if shelved for a time, will surely reappear.

Just as the recent evolution of the form of the urban mall can stand comparison with the earlier periods of arcade development, so also can its impact upon the structural arrangements of the surrounding city. Three projects from the expansive years of the mid-nineteenth century serve to illustrate the way in which the invention of enclosed pedestrian space on a large scale was seen in the past to have implications far beyond the local circumstances of retailing. All three were for central London, and, although none was ever built, they were studiously costed, enthusiastically received and seriously debated at the time, and, even in the context of the skywalk systems and the largest redevelopment projects of the past twenty years, remain extraordinarily ambitious in their scope. The first, by Gye, in 1845, envisaged a continuous sequence of arcades, crescents and rotundas raised on arches above the existing streets, and extending from the City to Trafalgar Square. A glazed arcade, 21 metres high and flanked by shops, was to extend the length of this structure, expanding in places to accommodate a flower market and 'several magnificent galleries, or halls'.[3] This was followed by William Moseley's plan of 1855 for the Crystal Way, a structure of

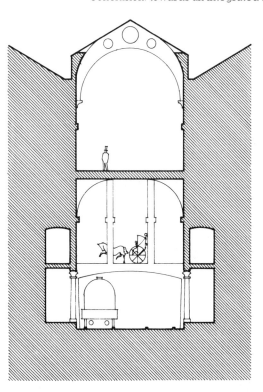

9.3 Crystal Way Project, London: cross-section. 1 : 300.

elaborate cross-section [9.3], with a pedestrian arcade raised above an underground railway, which was to describe a great loop, 3.8 kilometres long, running from St Paul's to Oxford Street, down Regent Street to Trafalgar Square, and back to the City along the Strand. Finally, and in the same year, Joseph Paxton proposed an adaptation of his Crystal Palace section to solve London's circulation problems in a single dramatic structure, The Great Victorian Way, describing an even wider loop, 16 kilometres long and connecting all the main-line termini which ring the city centre. Within an arcade space 22 metres wide and 35 metres high, a pedestrian way at ground level was to be surmounted by four express and four local railway lines in enclosed side galleries, and flanked by a mixture of commercial, residential and leisure uses according to the districts through which it passed.

Now these projects, neither 'ideal' in the sense of being purely theoretical solutions, nor entirely practical in the context of London, could be taken forward in two ways. On the one hand, and taking the sweeping diagram of their plans, they could lead to thorough-going exercises in the comprehensive reform of the circulation of the city, and on the other, taking the complexity of their section, they could point to the development of mall systems on a more elaborate scale. With each succeeding period of economic expansion, and most of all in the post-war years, both of these directions have been pursued with increasing enthusiasm, the first in theoretical planning proposals for the definitive reconstruction of the city, and the second

165

in the built examples of the urban mall. They have also been pursued as two entirely independent lines of inquiry, the first containing almost no references to the second, and the second being implemented often in spite of and in opposition to the policies of the first.

If we look at the classic planning projects which were produced at the same time as the shopping mall was undergoing its post-war development in disused airfields, old town centres and suburban lots across Europe and North America, the degree to which the attempted integration in the London projects of the questions of a rational urban structure of movement and of a new order of enclosed public space, had become split, is dramatically apparent. The former is now the reserve of public enterprise and the problem most likely to engage 'serious' architects and planners, whose explanations are couched in terms of 'efficiency' and 'society', while the latter is undertaken by private enterprise, by 'commercial' architects, and discussed in terms of 'economics' and 'consumers'. A great deal of discussion, analysis and criticism has been applied to the former,[4] and it is only necessary here to note their common assumption that urban structure was an autonomous creation, derived primarily from the vehicular network. Bluntly, 'urban motorways . . . form the structure of the community',[5] since, as the Smithsons saw it, 'the needs of the new mobile society and the communications systems which serve it invalidate existing town planning techniques of fixed building hierarchies and anonymous space', and therefore, 'the first step is to realise a system of urban motorways. Not just because we need more roads but because only they can make our cities an extension of ourselves as we now wish to be.'[6] This 'extension of ourselves' was not simply

a functional structure, like the sewers and utility networks, but also a symbolic one, which was made dramatically visible by the dissolution of extraneous features on the ground upon which it was laid out. In this respect, the International Planning Competition of 1958 for the centre of Berlin presented an ideal opportunity since, as Le Corbusier (1965:230) noted, 'there had been no hesitation: no need to pull down master-works of the past in order to rebuild. The demolition had been performed by aeroplanes and nothing was left standing in the centre of Berlin.' Thus, in both his proposal [9.4] and the Smithsons' [9.5], the iconic diagram of circulation as structure could stand, clean and free, against a blank ground, as if the fluid imagery of these projects, of 'flow' and 'stream' which had been poetically evoked in Louis Kahn's analogy of harbours and rivers for the circulation of Philadelphia [9.6], had washed over the whole city, leaving islands of habitation disposed upon the liberated circulation structure. This watery metaphor became physical fact in Kenzo Tange's 1960 plan for the expansion of Tokyo across Tokyo Bay, in which the site was finally dissolved away, to expose the city structure as a skeleton of circulation routes to which component buildings might be attached [9.7].

The assumption that urban structure, and with it public space, is something imposed from outside upon the accommodation functions of the city, which may be regarded as more or less specialised components plugged into the frame, rather than as something which is generated outwards from the accommodation functions themselves, was common to planning concepts of the period. Thus Nicholas Habraken (1972), beginning from a rather different philosophical position from Le Corbusier, for example, nevertheless concluded that the

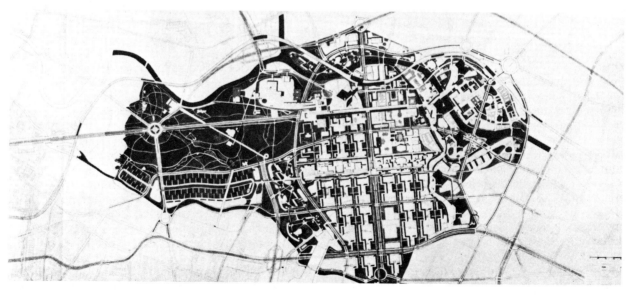

9.4 Competition for replanning the centre of Berlin, 1958: plan of Le Corbusier's proposal.

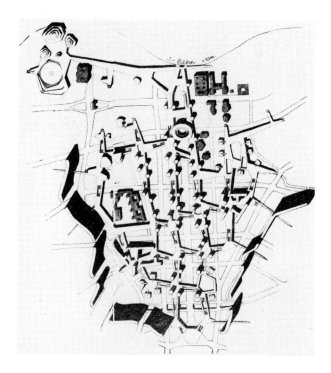

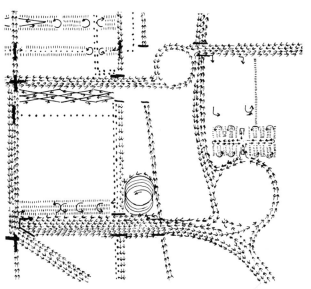

9.6 Louis Kahn: diagram of vehicular movements as the flow of water in his planning proposals for Philadelphia, 1952.

9.5 Berlin competition: plan of A. and P. Smithsons' proposal.

appropriate function of the public planner was to create, literally, urban structure, in the form of 'support structures' within which the private developer would be free to create his own enclosures, presumably without any 'structural' implications for surrounding developments.

Now in this book we have confined our attention to that other descendant of the London arcade projects, the shopping mall as actually built, and have suggested that, despite its variety, its expediency and its lack of theoretical programme, it nevertheless embodies a remarkably consistent form of urban structure, and one which is different from both that of the future city which the Ville Radieuse and its post-war variants proposed to create, and that of the existing city which they sought to replace.

This structure can be summarised in a simple diagram of primary pedestrian routes, spaced about 200 metres apart (an alternative triangulated network, as described in Chapter 7, is also possible) and with primary node spaces formed at their intersections [9.8]. It can be read in two ways, both as a diagram of circulation (the network of routes) [9.9], and as a diagram of functional organisation, in which dominant functions in terms of access to pedestrian frontage cluster at the node points, and establish a functional hierarchy within the area extending out 100 metres in all directions (the functional cell) [9.10]. Depending upon the intensity of development, secondary points of focus and access can develop at the intermediate midpoints in the network [9.11].

9.7 Kenzo Tange: model of proposals for Tokyo Bay, 1960.

Most of the centre plans which have been discussed approximate to this pattern of circulation and functional organisation. In the case of the out-of-town centres, the absence of site constraints permitted the free development of string sequences, as at Parly 2 [9.12], Yorkdale [9.13] and North Park [9.14], or circuits, as at Scarborough [9.15], which created variations with the disposition of primary and secondary node spaces, all of which could be read as specific interpretations of excerpts from the generic pattern in response to the

167

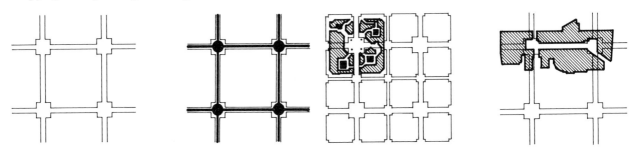

9.8 Diagram of primary network of pedestrian routes and squares. 1 : 12,000 (left).
9.9 Diagram can be read as a system of circulation (right).

9.16 Le Complexe Desjardins overlaid on base diagram (left).
9.17 Victoria Centre overlaid on base diagram (right).

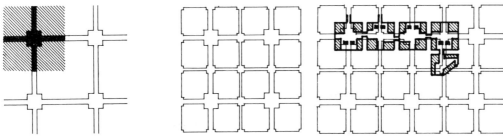

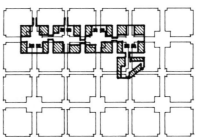

9.10 or as a cellular pattern of organisation, based upon the node squares (left).
9.11 The primary diagram can be intensified by intermediate nodes and routes (right).

9.18 Embarcadero Center overlaid on base diagram.

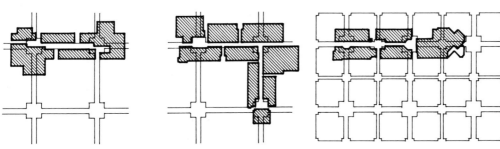

9.12 Parly 2 overlaid on base diagram (left).
9.13 Yorkdale overlaid on base diagram (right).

9.19 Eaton Centre overlaid on base diagram.

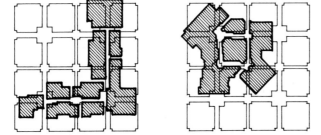

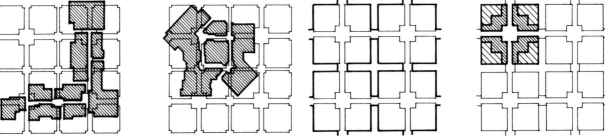

9.14 North Park overlaid on base diagram (left).
9.15 Scarborough Town Centre overlaid on base diagram (right).

9.20 Transformation of city pattern into net of development cells (left).
9.21 Hierarchy of functions within each cell according to need for access to perimeter or centre (right).

particular development brief. For those centres built on existing urban sites, one would expect the development of the pattern to be constrained by the circumstances of the former block form, highly irregular in the case of the British examples, or to a predetermined grid in most North American cities. Nevertheless it recurs as a persistent underlying feature of these mall plans also, whether as a single complete cell, as at Santa Monica Place, Le Complexe Desjardins [9.16] or, in England, St Albans, or as an extended sequence, as in the Victoria Centre [9.17] and Embarcadero Center [9.18]. And where the amalgamation of several city blocks allowed the formation of a continuous development, as at the Eaton Centre, this was articulated in accordance with the diagram [9.19].

In terms of the impact of this pattern upon the existing city, its effect was to displace open traffic streets to the interstices of the cellular organisation, and, as has been noted, to reverse the customary relationships of frontage and value. The centres which have been discussed can be seen as partial transformations of the city pattern into this form, the end result of which would be a net of development cells bounded by the vehicular street system, and linked by the pedestrian mall network [9.20]. The structure of each cell would define, not only paths of movement, but also hierarchies of function within it, depending upon the need of each use for access to the pedestrian, enclosed spaces of the centre or vehicular, open spaces of the perimeter [9.21].

The specific effect of this transformation in a particular city will then depend upon its circumstances. In many of the English examples, as at Chester [9.22], or St Albans, the scale of development is such as to maintain active frontage in both conditions and thus to appear as little more than a benign intensification of the former state. But where the existing block pattern is too small to allow the full cell to develop within it, a more dramatic reversal occurs. Thus in the centre of Houston, where the street grid is set out at approximately 100-metre intervals, the creation of a focus at the centre of each block absorbs the whole capacity of the pattern and there could be little opportunity for such coexistence [9.23].

It has been suggested here that this development pattern is reminiscent of archaic forms of pedestrian-based cities, discernible in medieval towns, and notably Venice, and last evident in Newcourt and Oglethorpe's proposals for parish or ward-based city plans [9.24]. Its reappearance through the agency of the urban mall creates a challenge for urban planning which has hardly begun to be resolved. As a system of circulation, it implies a continuous network of pedestrian spaces, regarded not as concessions by individual developers, but as the most public, active and, in a philosophical rather than an environmental sense, 'open' parts of the city, with all the problems of co-operation and control which that suggests. As a

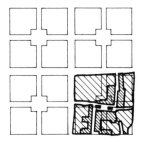

9.22 Grosvenor Centre, Chester, as version of development cell occupying the south-east quadrant of Chester's Roman plan.

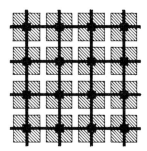

9.23 Diagrammatic plan of centre of Houston, to same scale (1 : 12,000). The pattern is constrained by the relatively small, 100-metre-square, street grid.

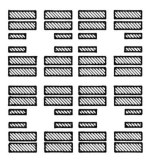

9.24 Savannah, Georgia: plan of four ward units to the same scale.

system of functional organisation it implies a mixed pattern of uses in which the potential of each condition of the cell form is realised, and again this raises difficulties. For, even where the site depth has permitted the full growth of a cell unit, the tendency has been to push its service functions, and particularly car parking and the rear walls of deep shop units, to the perimeter, 'killing' the street. For both street and mall systems to survive as effective public spaces, the development of appropriate perimeter uses, such as residential and office accommodation, requiring the light, air and individual vehicle access which the interior mall does not provide, must evolve in parallel with those within.

Some recent planning studies have indicated the ways in which the two aspects, of circulation and functional organisation, implicit in this pattern might be developed. The 'Ideplan 77' proposals for central Copenhagen, for example, prepared by the Danish Institut for Center-Planlaegning,[7] have applied the principle of back-land development to provide a comprehensive, but low-key, strategy for the city centre along these lines. Devised in the context of the relative decline in the dominance of central Copenhagen in relation to its hinterland, which had been reinforced by the planned dispersal of much of its employment and retailing to outer areas, the plan envisaged the creation of 'part-cities' defined by vehicular streets, within which pedestrian lanes would lead to reconstructed back-land development of building and pedestrian squares in the centres of these blocks [9.25]. Intended to even out land values within a block, at present declining sharply inward from the perimeter, and to extend the pedestrian street system based on the Strøget on a wider scale [9.26], the scheme suggested that individual part-cities would develop a specialised emphasis, not in terms of single land-use zoning, but in terms of broader themes which provide the continued

attraction of the city centre. Thus one part-city would act as a 'theme-centre' for music/radio/television, and another for film/photo/books/theatre, and so on, and each would comprise a mix of retail, eating, residential, performance and work spaces appropriate to its specialism.

This interpretation of the parochial cell as theme-centre was thus an attempt both to reinterpret the pattern of land-use in a city centre whose functional significance in the city region was in decline, and at the same time to establish a structural rationale for the piecemeal extension of its burgeoning pedestrianisation system. Another study, prepared by Design Teaching Practice for the central area of Telford New Town in England[8] illustrated the application of similar principles to the problems of unpredictable patterns of growth. The experience of earlier British New Towns had demonstrated the difficulties of sustaining comprehensive design concepts for the central area over the time-span of twenty or more years in which development would occur. The most consistent solutions, as at Milton Keynes and Runcorn, were those in which the bulk of construction had occurred in a single phase, while those with protracted development programmes, as at Cumbernauld, had suffered an obsolescence of design principles far more rapid than that of the buildings they had engendered. In the more pessimistic economic climate of 1976, when the Telford proposals were framed, the unpredictable nature of future development, in terms of when it

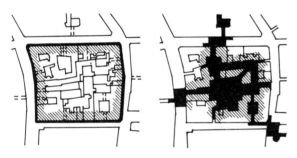

9.25 Ideplan 77, Copenhagen: transformation of a city block; before (left) and after (right). Pedestrian areas are shown solid black and prime frontage shown hatched. 1 : 3,000.

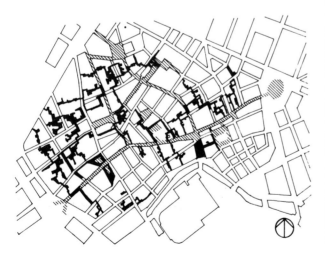

9.26 Ideplan 77, Copenhagen: proposals for the extension of the existing pedestrian areas (hatched) by the transformation of 'part-cities' (solid black). 1 : 12,000.

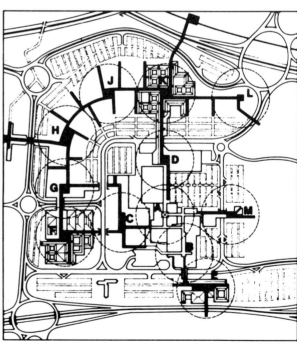

9.27 Telford New Town Centre: competition proposals by the Design Teaching Practice. Letters identify individual node-centred phasing packages of development.

would occur, what functions it would contain and what form it would take, had become a major design concern.

Like the Copenhagen Ideplan 77, the Telford proposal did not set out a land-use plan, nor indeed an urban design plan of future built form. Rather it laid down a future network of pedestrian routes [9.27], sheltered by free-standing canopy structures, and extending out from the malls which had already been built in the centre of the site. These routes were articulated by node places, which would form the foci of surrounding packages of development, each about 100 metres deep around the node point. Such a package was envisaged as a phasing unit, comprising the particular, and unforeseeable, mixture of uses called for at that stage in the development of the centre, and self-sufficient in terms of financing and viability, energy generation and usage, and urban design.

Whether such projects, attempting to apply the 'deep structure' of development engendered by the urban mall to the problems of the decline and growth of central areas, may have relevance for the future remains to be seen. What seems unavoidable is the fact that the seeds of that structure, in a thousand malls, arcades and precincts, have now been scattered throughout our cities. At present they conduct an unresolved debate with the quarters in which they lie, the outcome of which awaits the next period of economic growth.

Notes

1. Sussman, A., *Review of the American Scene*, paper to International Council of Shopping Centers 5th Annual European Conference, London 1980.

2. See Marriott, O., (1969) for a fascinating account of the history of the British developers.

3. Article by Gye in *The Builder*, 15 Dec. 1855:603f, quoted by Geist (1983).

4. See, for example, Gosling, D. and Maitland, B. (1984) for a review of post-war planning projects, and for a comprehensive bibliography of the subject.

5. London Roads Study, *Architectural Design*, May 1960.

6. Smithson, A. and P., 'Team 10 Primer 1953–62', *Architectural Design*, Dec. 1962:584, 586.

7. *Ideplan 77 for City*, published by Institut for Center-Planlaegning, Copenhagen 1977.

8. Finalist competition entry for town centre planning competition held by Telford Development Corporation, 1976.

Appendix: Data on principal centres

The following information on the principal shopping centre projects referred to in the text is provided, where known:

(a) location; (b) date of opening; (c) name of developer; (d) name of architect; (e) approximate gross retail leasable area, in square metres.

The centres are listed alphabetically, by country and, in the case of Canada and the USA, province or state.

Australia

- **Mid City Centre:** (a) Sydney, NSW, city centre, from Pitt to George Streets, between King and Market Streets; (b) 1982, (c) Gamgee Pty Ltd.; (d) Harry Seidler and Associates; (e) 8,000 sq. metres.
- **MLC Centre:** (a) Sydney, NSW, city centre, between Martin Place and King Street, and Castlereagh and Pitt Streets; (b) 1978; (c) The Mutual Life and Citizens Assurance Co. Ltd; (d) Harry Seidler and Associates; (e) 6,000 sq. metres.

Canada

ALBERTA

- **Housing Union Building:** (a) Edmonton, on 112th Street, between 89th and 92nd Street; (b) 1973; (d) A. J. Diamond and Barton Myers, with R. L. Wilkin; (e) 1,900 sq. metres.

ONTARIO

- **Don Mills Centre:** (a) Toronto, north-east suburbs, 9.5 kilometres from city centre on Lawrence Avenue and Don Mills Road; (b) 1954, refurbished 1978; (c) The Cadillac Fairview Corporation Ltd.
- **Eaton Centre:** (a) Toronto, city centre on Yonge Street between Queen and Dundas Streets; (b) 1977 and 1980; (c) The Cadillac Fairview Corporation Ltd; (d) Bregman and Hamann, and Craig Zeidler Strong; (e) 54,000 sq. metres.
- **Fairview Mall:** (a) Toronto, north-east suburbs, 14.5 kilometres from city centre on Sheppard Avenue and Don Valley Parkway; (b) 1970; (c) The Fairview Corporation Ltd; (d) Bregman and Hamann with Gruen Associates; (e) 52,000 sq. metres.
- **Oakville Place:** (a) Oakville, Trafalgar Road and Queen Elizabeth Way, 40 kilometres west of Toronto; (b) 1981; (c) Oxford Shopping Centres; (d) Petroff and Jeruzalski Architects with Cope Linder Associates; (e) 42,000 sq. metres.
- **Scarborough Town Centre:** (a) Scarborough, McCowan Road and MacDonald-Cartier Freeway (Highway 401); 19 kilometres north-east of Toronto Centre; (b) 1973 and 1979; (c) Trizec Equities Ltd; (d) Bregman and Hamann; (e) 100,000 sq. metres.
- **Sherway Gardens:** (a) Toronto, 14.5 kilometres west of city centre, at junction of Highway 427 and The Queensway Avenue in Mississauga; (b) 1971 and 1975; (c) The Rouse Company; (d) Fleiss and Murray; (e) 85,000 sq. metres.
- **Toronto-Dominion Centre:** (a) Toronto, city centre, Wellington Street and Bay Street; (b) 1967, 1969 and 1974; (c) The Cadillac Fairview Corporation Ltd; (d) Mies Van der Rohe; (e) 16,000 sq. metres.
- **Yorkdale Centre:** (a) Toronto, 8 kilometres north of city centre at junction of MacDonald-Cartier Freeway and William R. Allen Expressway; (b) 1964; (c) Trizec Equities Ltd, with Triton Centres and Simpsons Ltd; (d) John Graham and Associates, John B. Parkins Associates and Victor Gruen Design Associates; (e) 125,000 sq. metres.

QUEBEC

- **Le Complexe Desjardins:** (a) Montreal, city centre, between Rue Ste-Catherine and Rue Dorchester, and Rue Jeanne-Mance and Rue St-Urbain; (b) 1976; (c) Gouvernement du Québec, with Mouvement des Caisses Populaires Desjardins; (d) Blouin et Blouin, and Gauthier Guithé Roy; (e) 25,000 sq. metres.
- **Place Bonaventure:** (a) Montreal, city centre, between Rue de la Gauchetière and Rue St-Antoine, and Rue University and Rue Mansfield; (b) 1967; (c) Concordia Estates; (d) Affleck Desbarats Dimakopoulos Lebensold Sise; (e) 14,000 sq. metres.
- **Place Ville Marie:** (a) Montreal, city centre, Rue University and Rue Dorchester; (b) 1963; (c) Trizec Corporation; (d) I. M. Pei, with Henry N. Cobb, and Vincent Ponte; (e) 15,000 sq metres.
- **2020 University:** (a) Montreal, city centre, Boulevard de Maisonneuve and Rue University; (b) 1972; (c) Trizec Equities Ltd and Centre Metro Inc.; (d) Webb Zerafa Menkes Housden; (e) 8,000 sq. metres.

Denmark

- **Rodovre Centrum:** (a) Copenhagen, new town/suburb 16 kilometres west of city centre; (b) 1966; (c) A. Knudsen; (d) Krohn and Hartvig Rasmussen; (e) 30,000 sq. metres.

France

- **Belle Epine:** (a) Paris, 12 kilometres south of city centre, at junction of N7 and N186 at Rungis; (b) 1971; (c) SECAR-SEGECE; (d) Cabinet Colloc and Lathrop Douglass-Aaron Chelouche; (e) 92,000 sq. metres.
- **Creteil Soleil:** (a) Paris, 12 kilometres south-east of city centre, on Avenue du Général de Gaulle, Creteil; (b) 1974; (c) SEMAEC-SEGECE; (d) M. Dufav and Lathrop Douglass-Aaron Chelouche; (e) 93,000 sq. metres.
- **Forum des Halles:** (a) Paris, city centre, between Rue Saint Honoré and Rue Rambuteau, by the Jardin des Halles; (b) 1979; (c) SERETE Aménagement; (d) Vasconi and Pencreac'h; (e) 40,000 sq. metres.
- **Parly 2:** (a) Paris, 16 kilometres west of city centre on N184 at Le Chesnay; (b) 1969; (c) Société des Centres Commerciaux (SCC); (d) Lathrop Douglass-Aaron Chelouche, with Claude Balick; (e) 55,000 sq. metres.
- **La Part-Dieu:** (a) Lyons, city centre, east bank of Rhône, at Boulevard Vivier Merle and Boulevard E. Deruelle; (b) 1975; (c) SCC; (d) Charles Delfante, Régis Zeller and Copeland Novak and Israel; (e) 110,000 sq. metres.
- **Rosny 2:** (a) Paris, 10 kilometres east of city centre, at Rosny; (b) 1973; (c) SCC; (d) CNI International; (e) 83,000 sq. metres.

Germany

- **Calwer Strasse:** (a) Stuttgart, Rotebühlplatz and Theodor-Heuss-Strasse; (b) 1978; (d) Kammerer and Belz and Partner; (e) 5 400 sq. metres.

Sweden

- **Farsta New Town Centre:** (a) Farsta New Town, outside Stockholm; (b) 1960; (d) Sven Backstrom and Leif Reinius; (e) 40,000 sq. metres.

United Kingdom

- **Arndale Centre:** (a) Manchester, city centre, Cannon Street and Market Street; (b) 1976; (c) Town and City Properties Ltd; (d) Sir Hugh Wilson and Lewis Womersley; (e) 93,000 sq. metres.

- **Brent Cross:** (a) London, by junction of North Circular and M1; (b) 1976; (c) Hammerson Property and Investment Trust; (d) BEP Parnership; (e) 73,000 sq. metres.
- **Brunel Centre:** (a) Swindon, Wiltshire, town centre on Regent Street and Canal Walk; (b) 1973 to 1979; (c) Thamesdown District Council; (d) Douglas Stephen and Building Design Partnership; (e) 48,000 sq. metres.
- **Cofferidge Close:** (a) Stony Stratford, Milton Keynes, on High Street; (b) 1976; (c) Milton Keynes Development Corporation; (d) Milton Keynes Development Corporation; (e) 2,000 sq. metres.
- **Covent Garden Market:** (a) Covent Garden, London West End; (b) 1980; (c) The GLC Covent Garden Committee; (d) Historic Buildings Division, GLC Department of Architecture and Civic Design; (e) 5,000 sq. metres.
- **Coventry City Centre:** (a) Coventry, City centre; (b) 1955; (c) The city of Coventry; (d) the City Architect.
- **Eldon Square:** (a) Newcastle upon Tyne, 400 metres north of Central Station and Town Hall; (b) 1976; (c) Capital and Counties; (d) Chapman Taylor and Partners; (e) 72,500 sq. metres.
- **Grosvenor Centre:** (a) Chester, city centre behind Eastgate in south-east corner of walled area; (b) 1965; (c) Grosvenor Estate Commercial Developments Ltd; (d) Sir Percy Thomas and Partners; (e) 20,000 sq. metres.
- **Harlow New Town Centre:** (a) Harlow New Town; (b) 1956; (c) Harlow New Town Development Corporation; (d) Sir Frederick Gibberd and Partners.
- **Irvine New Town Centre:** (a) Irvine, Ayrshire, Scotland, adjoining west side of old town centre; (b) 1975; (c) Ravenseft Properties; (d) Irvine Development Corporation; (e) 23,000 sq. metres.
- **London Pavilion:** (a) London, Piccadilly Circus; (b) 1983; (c) The London Pavilion Company Ltd; (d) Chapman Taylor Partners; (e) 1,100 sq. metres.
- **Milton Keynes Shopping Centre:** (a) Milton Keynes, from M1 junction 14; (b) 1979; (c) Milton Keynes Development Corporation; (d) Milton Keynes Development Corporation; (e) 102,000 sq. metres.
- **Piece Hall:** (a) Halifax, West Yorkshire; (b) 1976; (c) Metropolitan Borough of Calderdale; (d) Metropolitan Borough of Calderdale, Architect's Department.
- **Quadrant Centre:** (a) Swansea, West Glamorgan, off Nelson Street; behind Oxford Street; (b) 1978; (c) CIN Properties, with local authority; (d) Building Design Partnership; (e) 28,000 sq. metres.
- **Queensgate Centre:** (a) Peterborough, city centre, on Westgate and Long Causeway; (b) 1982; (c) Norwich Union Life Insurance Society with Peterborough Development Corporation; (d) Peterborough Development Corporation; (e) 46,000 sq. metres.
- **The Ridings:** (a) Wakefield, Yorkshire, town centre on Kirkgate; (b) 1983; (c) Capital and Counties with Wakefield Metropolitan District Council; (d) Chapman Taylor Partners; (e) 23,000 sq. metres.
- **Runcorn Shopping City:** (a) Runcorn New Town Centre, Cheshire; (b) 1971; (c) Grosvenor Estate Commercial Developments; (d) Runcorn Development Corporation; (e) 56,000 sq. metres.
- **Victoria Centre:** (a) Nottingham, Parliament Street, city centre; (b) 1972; (c) Capital and Counties; (d) Arthur Swift and Partners; (e) 58,000 sq. metres.

- **Waterthorpe Centre:** (a) Mosborough, Sheffield, South Yorkshire, (b) in progress; (c) Chesterfield Properties PLC; (d) Building Design Partnership; (e) 35,000 sq. metres.
- **Waverley Market:** (a) Edinburgh, east end of Princes Street; (b) in progress; (d) Building Design Partnership.
- **West One:** (a) London, Oxford Street; (b) 1981; (c) MEPC; (d) Chapman Taylor Partners; (e) 4,000 sq. metres.
- **Whitgift Centre:** (a) Croydon, Surrey, town centre; (b) 1968; (c) Ravenseft Properties; (d) The Fitzroy Robinson Partnership.
- **Wood Green Shopping City:** (a) Wood Green, North London, on High Road; (b) 1980; (c) Electricity Supply Nominees and London Borough of Haringey; (d) Sheppard Robson Architects; (e) 44,000 sq. metres.

USA

CALIFORNIA

- **Broadway Plaza:** (a) Los Angeles, city centre, 7th Street and Hope Street; (b) 1973; (c) Plaza Development Associates; (d) The Luckman Partnership Inc.; (e) 36,000 sq. metres.
- **The Cannery:** (a) San Francisco, Fisherman's Wharf area, Jefferson and Leavenworth Street; (d) Esherick Homsey Dodge and Davis.
- **Eastridge Center:** (a) San Jose, Capitol Expressway and Quimby; (b) 1971; (c) Bayshore Properties and Homart; (d) Avner Naggar; (e) 130,000 sq. metres.
- **Embarcadero Centre:** (a) San Francisco, city centre, Sacramento Street and Drumm Street; (b) 1981; (c) John Portman, David Rockefeller, Prudential Insurance Co.; (d) John Portman and Associates; (e) 50,000 sq. metres.
- **Fox Hills Mall:** (a) Culver City, Los Angeles, San Diego Freeway and Marina del Ray Freeway; (b) 1975; (c) Ernest W. Hahn Inc.; (d) Gruen Associates; (e) 84,000 sq. metres.
- **Ghirardelli Square:** (a) San Francisco, Fisherman's Wharf area, North point and Larkin Street; (b) 1964; (c) William M. Roth; (d) Wurster, Bernadi and Emmons, with Lawrence Halprin and Associates; (e) 5,000 sq. metres.
- **Jack London Village:** (a) Oakland, Waterfront; (b) 1975; (d) Frank Laulainen and Associates; (e) 6,000 sq. metres.
- **Pier 39:** (a) San Francisco, Fisherman's Wharf area, Jefferson and Powell Street; (b) 1978; (c) W. L. Simmons; (d) Walker and Moody; (e) 19,000 sq. metres.
- **Plaza Pasadena:** (a) Pasadena, Los Angeles, Colorado Boulevard and Los Robles Avenue; (b) 1980; (c) Ernest W. Hahn Inc.; (d) Charles Kober Associates; (e) 70,000 sq. metres.
- **Ports O'Call:** (a) San Pedro, Los Angeles, Harbor Boulevard and 13th Street.
- **Prune Yard:** (a) San Jose, Bascom Avenue and Hamilton Avenue.
- **Santa Anita Fashion Park:** (a) Arcadia, Los Angeles, Huntingdon Drive and Baldwin Avenue; (b) 1974; (c) Ernest W. Hahn Inc.; (d) Gruen Associates; (e) 90,000 sq. metres.

- **Santa Monica Place:** (a) Santa Monica, Los Angeles, 2nd Street and Colorado; (b) 1980; (c) Santa Monica Place Associates, The Rouse Company, Ernest W. Hahn Inc.; (d) Frank O. Gehry and Associates, Gruen Associates; (e) 53,000 sq. metres.
- **Stanford Mall:** (a) Palo Alto, Arboretum Road, off El Camino Real and San Antonio Avenue; (b) 1978; (c) Stanford University; (d) Bull Field Volkmann Stockwell; (e) 114,000 sq. metres.
- **The Willows:** (a) Concord, Interstate 680, Willow Pass Road; (b) 1976; (c) Willow Concord Venture; (d) Leason Pomeroy; (e) 24,000 sq. metres.

GEORGIA

- **Peachtree Center:** (a) Atlanta, city centre, Sprint Street; (b) 1973; (c) John Portman; (d) John Portman Associates; (e) 22,000 sq. metres.

ILLINOIS

- **Lakehurst Centre:** (a) Waukegan, 56 kilometres north of Chicago, on Highway 41 and Belvidere; (b) 1971; (c) Arthur Rubloff and Company; (d) Gruen Associates; (e) 118,000 sq. metres.
- **Northbrook Centre:** (a) Northbrook, 32 kilometres north of centre of Chicago, on Lake Cook Road, east of junction with Highway 43; (b) 1976; (c) Homart Development Company; (d) Architectronics Inc.; (e) 106,000 sq. metres.
- **Old Orchard:** (a) Skokie, 21 kilometres north of centre of Chicago, on Edens Expressway, Highway 41; (b) 1956; (c) Urban Investment and Development Co.; (d) Loebl, Schlossman, Bennett and Dart; (e) 105,000 sq. metres.
- **Water Tower Place:** (a) Chicago, city centre, N. Michigan Avenue and Pearson Street; (b) 1976; (c) Urban Investment and Development Co.; (d) Loebl, Schlossman, Bennett and Dart, and C. F. Murphy Associates and Warren Platner Associates; (e) 55,000 sq. metres.
- **Woodfield Mall:** (a) Schaumburg, 40 kilometres west of centre of Chicago on Highways 72 and 53; (b) 1971; (c) Homart and Taubman; (d) Peter M. Tsolinas and Associates Inc., Larsen-Wulf Associates, Charles Luckman Associates; (e) 204,000 sq. metres.

INDIANA

- **The Commons:** (a) Columbus, town centre, Brown, Washington, 3rd and 44th Streets; (b) 1973; (d) Gruen Associates; (e) 10,000 sq. metres.

MARYLAND

- **Harborplace:** (a) Baltimore, Inner Harbor; (b) 1980; (c) The Rouse Company; (d) Benjamin Thompson and Associates; (e) 6,000 sq. metres.
- **The Mall in Columbia:** (a) Columbia, Warfield Parkway; (b) 1971 and 1981; (c) The Rouse Company; (d) Cope Linder; (e) 85,000 sq. metres.

- **White Marsh Center:** (a) Baltimore County, Exit 3 on Highway 95; (b) 1981; (c) The Rouse Company; (e) 107,000 sq. metres.

MASSACHUSETTS

- **Faneuil Hall:** (a) Boston, city centre, Congress Street and South Market; (b) 1976; (c) The Rouse Company; (d) Benjamin Thompson Associates; (e) 20,000 sq. metres.
- **The Mall at Chestnut Hill:** (a) Boston, 9.5 kilometres west of city centre at Hammond Street on Boylston Street; (b) 1974; (d) Sumner Schein; (e) 35,000 sq. metres.
- **Pickering Wharf:** (a) Salem, Derby Street.

MINNESOTA

- **Southdale:** (a) Minneapolis, York Street and 70th Street; (b) 1956; (d) Victor Gruen Associates; (e) 62,000 sq. metres.

NEVADA

- **The Plazas at First Western Square:** (a) Las Vegas, Sahara Avenue and Richfield Boulevard; (b)1980; (c) John H. Midby and Associates; (d) Paul Thoryle and Associates.

NEW YORK

- **The Galleria:** (a) White Plains, Main Street; (b) 1981; (c) Cadillac Fairview Shopping Centers (US) Ltd; (d) Copeland, Novak and Israel; (e) 80,000 sq. metres.
- **The Market at Citicorp:** (a) Manhattan, 54th Street and Lexington Avenue; (b) 1978; (c) Citicorp; (d) Hugh Stubbins and Associates; (e) 6,000 sq. metres.

PENNSYLVANIA

- **The Gallery at Market East:** (a) Philadelphia, city centre, 9th and Market Streets; (b) 1977; (c) The Rouse Company and the Redevelopment Authority of the city of Philadelphia; (d) Bower and Fradley Architects; Cope Linder Associates; (e) 19,000 sq. metres.
- **New Market:** (a) Philadelphia, Society Hill area, 2nd, Pine, Lombard and Front Streets, (b) 1975, altered 1978; (c) Van Arkel Moss; (d) Louis Sauer and Charles Broudy and Associates; (e) 4,000 sq. metres.

TEXAS

- **Galleria:** (a) Houston, 8 kilometres west of city centre at Westheimer Road off West Loop South Freeway; (b) Phase I 1970, Phase II 1977; (c) Gerald D. Hines; (d) Hellmuth, Obata and Kassabaum; (e) 73,000 sq. metres.
- **Hulen Mall:** (a) Fort Worth; (b) 1977; (d) Hellmuth, Obata and Kassabaum; (e) 48,000 sq. metres.

Appendix: Data on principal centres

- **North Park:** (a) Dallas; (b) 1964; (d) Harrell and Hamilton.

VIRGINIA

- **Crystal Underground Village:** (a) Arlington, Crystal City on Highway 1; (b) 1980; (c) Charles E. Smith.

WISCONSIN

- **Mayfair Center:** (a) Milwaukee; (b) 1959; (c) Froedtert-Mayfair; (d) Perkins and Will, Grassold-Johnson and Associates; (e) 100,000 sq. metres.

Bibliography

Adburgham, A. (1964) *Shops and Shopping, 1800–1914.* London.

Alexander, C., Ishikawa S., Silverstein M. et al. (1977) *A Pattern Language.* Oxford U.P., New York.

Beddington, N. (1982) *Design for Shopping Centres.* Butterworth Scientific, London.

Berry, B. J. L. (1967) *Geography of Market Centers and Retail Distribution.* Prentice-Hall Inc., Englewood Cliffs, N. J.

Bloomer, K.C. and **Moore, C. W.** (1977) *Body, Memory and Architecture.* Yale U. P., New Haven.

Brambilla, R. and **Longo, G.** (1977) *For Pedestrians Only: Planning, Design and Management of Traffic-Free Zones.* Whitney Library of Design, New York.

Conzen, M. R. G. (1960) *Alnwick, Northumberland: A Study in Town-plan Analysis.* Institute of British Geographers, London.

Dahl, W. H.(1980) 'Methods of slashing energy use are plentiful', *Shopping Centers Today*, May 1980.

Darlow, C. (1972) *Enclosed Shopping Centres.* Architectural Press, London.

Davies, R. L. and **Bennison, D. J.** (1979) *British Town Centre Shopping Schemes: A Statistical Digest*, URPI Ull. The Unit for Retail Planning Information, London.

Davies, R. L. and **Champion, A. G.** (eds) (1983) *The Future for The City Centre.* Academic Press, London.

Design for Modern Merchandising (1954), An Architectural Record Book. F. W. Dodge Corporation, New York.

Design for Shopping (1970). Capital and Countries Property Company Ltd, London.

Forusz, H. N. (1981) 'The Cincinnati Skywalk, Cincinnati, Ohio: A case study from the viewpoint of users and Public Authorities', *Contact: Journal of Urban and Environmental Affairs*, University of Waterloo, Canada, Vol. 13, no. 2/3, 1981, pp. 335–52.

Francaviglia, R. V. (1974) 'Main Street revisited', *Places*, vol. 1, no. 3, Oct. 1974: 7–11.

Fritz, J. (1894) Deutsche Stadtanlangen, *Beilage zum Programm 520 des Lyzeums Strassburg.* Strasburg.

Bibliography

Geist, J. F. (1983) *Arcades: The History of a Building Type.* MIT Press, Cambridge, Mass.
Goldenberg, S. (1981) *Men of Property: The Canadian Developers Who Are Buying America.* Personal Library, Toronto.
Gosling, D. and **Maitland, B.** (1976) *Design and Planning of Retail Systems.* Architectural Press, London.
Gosling, D. and **Maitland, B.** (1984) *Concepts of Urban Design.* Academy Editions, London.
Gradmann, R. (1914) *Die Stadtischen Siedlungen des Königreichs Württemberg.* Stuttgart.
Gruen, N. (1978) 'Gestalt magnetism or what is special about specialty shopping centers?' *Urban Land*, Jan. 1978: 3–9.
Gruen, V. and **Smith L.** (1960) *Shopping Towns USA: The Planning of Shopping Centers.* Reinhold, New York.

Habraken, N. J. (1972) *Supports: An Alternative to Mass Housing* (trans. B. Valkenburg). Architectural Press, London. (First published in Holland, 1961.)
Hines, M. A. (1983) *Shopping Center Development and Investment.* Wiley, New York.

Irvin, L. M. and **Groy, J. B.** (1982) *The Minneapolis Skyway System: what it is and why it works.* City Planning Department, Minneapolis.

Jacobs, J. (1961) *The Death and Life of Great American Cities.* Penguin, Harmondsworth.

Koolhaas, R. (1978) *Delirious New York: a retroactive manifesto for Manhattan.* Oxford U. P., New York.
Kornbluth, J. (1979) 'The department store as theater', *New York Times Magazine*, 29 Apr. 1979: 30–72.
Krier, R. (1979) *Urban Space.* Academy Editions, London.

Le Corbusier (1927) *Towards a New Architecture.* Architectural Press, London (trans. by Etchells, F. from *Vers une Architecture*, Editions Crès, Paris, 1923).
Le Corbusier (1961) *Oeuvre Complète, 1938–1946.* W. Boesiger aux Editions Girsberger, Zurich.
Le Corbusier (1965) *Oeuvre Complète, 1957–65.* Thames & Hudson, London.
Le Corbusier (1967) *The Radiant City.* Faber and Faber, London (trans. of *La Ville Radieuse*, Editions Vincent, Paris).
Le Corbusier (1971) *The City of Tomorrow.* Architectural Press, London (trans. by Etchells, F. from *Urbanisme*, Editions Crès, Paris 1924).
Lion, E. (1976) *Shopping Centers: Planning, Development and Administration.* Wiley, New York.
Lynch, K. (1960) *The Image of the City.* MIT Press, Cambridge, Mass.

Maitland, B. S. (1981) 'Buildings update: retailing', *The Architects' Journal*, 13 May 1981: 911–22; 20 May 1981: 959–71; 27 May 1981: 1021–31.
Marriott, O. (1969) *The Property Boom.* Pan, London.
Martin, P. G. (1982) *Shopping Centre Management.* E. & F. N. Spon, London.
Mumford, L. (1961) *The City in History.* Penguin, Harmondsworth.
Mun, D. (1981) *Shops: A Manual of Planning and Design.* Architectural Press, London.

Norberg-Schulz, C. (1971) *Existence, Space and Architecture.* Studio Vista, London.

Northern, R. and **Haskoll, M.** (1977) *Shopping Centres: A Developer's Guide to Planning and Design.* Centre for Advanced Land Use Studies, Reading.

Redstone, L. G. (1973) *New Dimensions in Shopping Centers and Stores.* McGraw-Hill, New York.
Reps, J. W. (1965) *The Making of Urban America.* Princeton U.P., Princeton, N. J.
Rowe, C. and **Koetter, F.** (1978) *Collage City.* MIT Press, Cambridge, Mass.

Saxon, R. (1983) *Atrium Buildings.* Architectural Press, London.
Scott, N. K. (1980) 'Rebuilding town centres', *Estates Gazette*, vol. 254, 19 April 1980: 181–5.
Scott, N. K. and **Gammie, R.** (1979) 'Speciality centres'. *Estates Gazette*, vol. 251, 18 July, 1979: 353–5.
Shopping for Pleasure (1969). Capital and Counties Property Company Ltd, London.
Sitte, C. (1945) *The Art of Building Cities.* Reinhold, New York (trans. by Stewart, C. T. from *Der Städtebau nach seinen künstlerischen Grundsätzen*, Vienna, 1889).
Stephens, S. (1978) 'Introversion and the urban context', *Progressive Architecture*, Dec. 1978: 49–53.
Stirling, J. (1975) *James Stirling: Buildings and Projects 1950–1974.* Thames & Hudson, London.
Sutcliffe, A. (1970) *The Autumn of Central Paris; The Defeat of Town Planning 1850–1970.* Edward Arnold, London.

Thompson, J. McC. (1979) 'Boston's Faneuil Hall', *Urban Design International*, Nov./Dec. 1979, vol. 1, no. 1.

Whitehand, J. W. R. (ed.) (1981) *The Urban Landscape: Historical Development and Management. Papers by M. R. G. Conzen.* Academic Press, London.

Zeidler, E. H. (1983) *Multi-use Architecture in the Urban Context.* Karl Krämer Verlag, Stuttgart.

Index

(Shopping centres are indicated in *italic script*)